I WANT A GLASS OF WATER:

stories of surviving mother

Hope Doran

I WANT A GLASS OF WATER: stories of surviving mother

© 2023 Jessica Hope Doran

All rights reserved. No part of this book may be reproduced in any form without permission in writing from the author. Reviewers may quote brief passages in reviews.

No part of this publication may be reproduced or transmitted in any form or by any means, mechanical or electronic, including photocopying or recording, or by any information storage and retrieval system, or transmitted by email without permission in writing from the author.

Neither the author nor the publisher assumes any responsibility for errors, omissions, or contrary interpretations of the subject matter herein. Any perceived slight of any individual or organization is purely unintentional.

To ensure privacy and confidentiality, the names and other identifying characteristics of the persons included in this book have been changed. All the personal examples of my own life and experiences have not been altered.

ISBN 978-1-961185-20-3 (hardcover)

Cover Design, Editing & Layout: Megs Thompson – megswrites llc
www.megswrites.com

www.inomniaparatuspublishing.com

SPECIAL THANKS...

To my loving wife who helped and encouraged me.

To Vinnie, my ever-present muse.

To my children, Ian, Vinnie, and Sam. You eternally have my love always.

To my beloved brother and sister-in-law, who read through the pain.

To David, may your mind expand its horizons through your granddaughter.

This is my story as I recall it. I put this book together in honor of both myself, and my children. It has not been put together with the idea of hurting others, but rather in part to help in my healing process. This story does not tell of my entire childhood, but the moments that scarred or traumatized me. I tell you of the moments that made me question my worth, my existence, and my ability to be loved. The events are as I recall them or, in part as stories were told to me regarding my younger years. There are chapters that, for the ease of reading and writing I combined several incidents into one, easier to follow chapter.

This wasn't just written for me. It was also written in the hope of helping others who have either gone through or are currently in similar life circumstances. I understand that my family members and others in this book, or in my life may voice different opinions or remembrances regarding my series of events. However, the events that I tell within my life's story are mine as I recall them. Their memories are theirs, and these memories are mine.

TABLE OF CONTENTS

Foreword 1

A Birth 5

I Want a Glass of Water 9

Flush! 13

Locked In 15

Pool Time 19

I Swear 21

Matches 23

Adrenaline Rush 29

Where's Hope? 33

Grandma 41

Who's Important? 47

Bathroom Time 53

Weight, What? 57

Missing Bike 61

Happy Birthday! 67

To Grandma's House I Go 71

Clean Your Room 75

Church 79

Missionettes 83

My Clothes 87

Please Smoke 91

Drama 97

The Biggest Lie 101

Camp 113

Volleyball	121
Vinyl on Fire	125
Dear Diary	131
Speaking in Tongues	135
Family	139
Mommy Dearest	143
Cat Food	147
Borrowing	151
Cynthia	157
Dooms Day	161
Sneaking Out	165
The Lengths Mother Would Go To	171
Get Out	185
Chicken Pox	191
A Hypothesis	195
College	199
Celebration	203
Does it Really Matter?	207
Brian	211
Graduation	217
Loss	221
Pregnancy	227
The Wedding	235
Unapproved Shopping	239
An End	247
Those People	251
Spanking	257
The Blanket	261

It's Better Than a House!	265
The Cutting Board	271
Koshi	275
Official	281
Alisa	285
Meeting Mother	289
Vinnie	293
Mother	299
Thoughts	305

FOREWORD

I remember when I found out I was to be a mother I was terrified. Sure, there was the unknown of pregnancy, whether I would be a good mom, a single mother, and how I would fare with all the changes that were about to occur. Not to mention how my body would change, or the emotional rollercoaster I would endure from being pregnant. None of these were what terrified me the most. What terrified me was the concern that I would be the same type of mother as the one I had.

I was engulfed in tragic moments shared with my mother, mean things that were said, the standards that were unattainable, the raging manipulation I endured, and the ever-present weight that I was never good enough. I say all this knowing she has her own version of who I was, and to be fair, I was not easy. However, I was molded by what I was given to work with.

I speak only of her not because my Father was not around, but because he chose not to use his voice. He did not protect me. He chose silence to ease his own burden. In doing so, he became Mother's puppet, and just as responsible for her actions as she was herself. His silence was a cloak that I wore for decades thinking the stillness of my voice was my only option. If he ever stood up for me, to this day I am unaware of it. I had suffered through countless encounters with Mother, listening to her spin her translation of them among her peers, gasping at how starkly different our realities were, but too afraid to confront her on them... until now.

My world starkly changed one crisp November evening. I hadn't talked with my mother in several years outside of my attempts to reach out to her on birthdays, holidays, and a few occasions when I simply missed her. Yes, you read that right. Despite everything, I missed her. Perhaps not her, but the idea of what she could be, what we could be. I had glimpses into that person throughout my life. It was what kept me coming back for so many years. The problem for me was that she was just not normally available. But oh, how I longed to have that!

That night in November, I needed it more than ever before. I was suffering a loss that gutted me. It was the wreckage of the moment that I reached out to her, seeking out what any daughter truly wants from her mother in a time of need. It was in that moment she denied me one last time. I mourned her loss as if she'd actually passed away. I mourned the death of any possible relationship with her. Her unwillingness to have one of those rare moments when she was what I truly wanted and needed permeated every crevice of my being. I mourned the loss of any possible repair or reconciliation. She obliterated me one last time before I finally decided I was worth more than what she had told me I was or had expressed that I was. It was that moment, after all these years, when I realized I was letting her define who I was, what I was worth, and if I was worth loving as a daughter. In that moment, I restored my own self-worth, and accepted that I didn't need her love to be whole. Restored, as in to be made whole, or complete. To strip away that which is old and no longer benefits me. I find peace in the word restored.

    We all start our lives untainted by others. We are whole and complete in who we are at birth. All parents paint on their children's canvas of life. Some provide positive brush strokes, while others, like my mother, paint in negative strokes. As children, we are given different interpretations of what is expected of us in our lives, and more paint is deposited over the last, creating complexities for us to work through as we mature. It is never presented to us that we can simply throw away those expectations, ideas, and notions of who we are based on what we're told by our parents. It's unfortunate, because too often we grow into adults assuming that it is just a part of us when in fact, it is not. My canvas had grown black and ugly with what Mother chose to paint on mine. I finally had the emotional strength to tell her no more. To rebuke her for attempting to create such an ugly portrait of me in my life, and then claim I had no choice but to accept it. I have reclaimed my canvas and am instead creating what I want out of the life I have been given to live.

    I wonder if a challenge is coming my way. I wonder if Father will find his voice, and if so, who will he defend? I wonder if Mother will read this at some point and become enraged. I want her anger to be over the realization of what was lost, but sadly, I don't foresee that. I see a woman who will retaliate with more hate, saying I was the evil one. Maybe to her I was, but I know that is not who I am, and I write this knowing that. I write this to set myself free. I have hidden my story all this time in the hope I would obtain a loving relationship with my mother. I will hide no longer, because there is nothing to shield, nothing to save. I share my story to set myself free from her entangled grasp and accept that there is nothing she can offer but the narrow-minded world she's tried to burden me with my entire life. I set myself free with my words, my story, and my survival into acceptance of who I am.

This memoir is part of my healing journey. It is putting into words those parts of my life that I felt were broken and ugly but were actually molding me into this beautiful soul that I hold as mine. I am strong. I am a warrior. I am kind, compassionate, and loving. I hope this will bring my healing to a close. I hope those who read this will find ways to do better by their daughters and sons. I hope some who read this will find healing from the mothers and fathers who can't or won't acknowledge. Denial is after all part of the framework of the narcissist. This book is dedicated to all who read it and walk away better for it.

A BIRTH

My parents were young when they had me, both still in their teens. To say they were unprepared would be an understatement. My father came from a working-class family, consisting of three children, and what I had been told was a very loving familial relationship. Mother came from an affluent family. She also had siblings, and from what I was told, seemed to be more of a business model for family dynamics than a loving one. That's not to say she came from a loveless family, just that it seemed love was not a priority within it. My mother was six years old when she lost her own mother to cancer. I can't help but wonder if that was a large part of what shaped my mother to be the person she was and continues to be. I know that for most of my life it's what gave me a plethora of grace when it came to how she treated me and the hateful things that were said.

That being said, things get to a point when, as an individual we all make choices to be who we are. We have those moments when we decide to better ourselves, protect ourselves, or isolate ourselves. All of those come with a cost, even the right choices can be hard learning moments, and oftentimes some sort of personal sacrifice is the price that's paid. Either it's for the betterment of self, or the more animalistic preservation of self. All this assuming the individual is of sound mind. I believe Mother's loss of her own did more than scar her. I believe it cut her deeply emotionally and mentally. I was the caveat that unleashed all the damage that was done within her. Rather than seeking out the help she so desperately needed for herself, she poured out all her pain, anguish, and disruptive mental fractures onto me.

For years I dealt with my mother just as she was. All in the hopes of gaining her acceptance and love. I have seen that in addition to mental health, a component of Mother's essence is that she is a narcissist. I did not know what a narcissist was until adulthood. Even then it was years before I attached that label to my mother, let alone the possible label of one suffering from mental health. Please understand that I am no doctor. My observation of Mother's mental state is purely based on a lifetime of interaction with her and my own road to mental health as a result. Even with my knowledge, I sought to protect her in the hopes of gaining her love. I'm talking about real love, not the fake "I love because I have to love this kid," kind of love. My reality was more on par with feeling that she loathed and resented me rather than loved me. I thought if I just loved her hard enough, and long enough, she would become who I desperately needed. I reached a point where I had to let go of that for my own sanity.

For that reason, I eventually had to change how I addressed the Mother who gave birth to me, and the Father who stood in the corners of the treachery I endured. Gone were the terms of endearment in calling them mom and dad. Instead, I embraced something they disliked. As a joke, my brother had called them the parental units. The distain of that title was so evident on Mother's face that it was palpable. She sharply retorted that she did not want to be referred to as a parental unit, stating that the term sounded sterile and cold. It is for that reason, I embrace the term parental units when referring to both Mother and Father. For although Father was silent, his silence impacted me just as heavily as Mother's scathing words and actions. This is me, calling back a small piece of power with regards to my childhood, and their privilege (whether or not they see it) of calling me their daughter.

As the story of my birth goes, my mother says she began having contractions in the early morning, so she and my father loaded up in their car and drove to the hospital. Upon arrival, my mother was wedged within the vehicle in such a way that she could not exit the car. It took several people, and a few harrowing minutes to free her and usher her to the hospital building.

Mother spoke of how difficult the birth was. She said it was traumatizing in and of itself, but additionally, they kept trying to bring her the wrong baby. She said she became enraged over this as it happened several times. The nurse told her it would be easier if she and my father would decide on a name. There were several names that had been kicked around, but according to my mother, she and my father would fight over it to the point they would just stop talking. So finally, they named me, but according to Mother, the switching of babies continued. Mother went so far as to tell me that even if I wasn't her biological child, I was hers by this point. I was in my 20's when she said this. To look at our family, there was no denying we were all related. My brother and I look like a blending of both our parents, as well as each other. When I responded by telling her this, she told me "Well, you never know, but I want you to know it doesn't matter."

It did matter. It mattered to me. In that moment she verbally gut-punched me, and then tried to give me symbolic flowers to make up for it, just like any other abusive relationship. There was no need to say I might not be biologically hers, yet she still chose to. Perhaps she thought of it as a possible reason why I was so difficult. Perhaps it was her own internal way of finding an excuse for her lack of love for me. Perhaps it was just a mean thing to say. Whatever the reason may have been, from the beginning it seemed as though my mother was looking for a way to excuse herself from being loving towards me.

Regardless, she said I was named Hope because the parental units had a lot of hope for me. Hope for what I would be, the things I would do, the kind of person I would grow to be. Hope for being a positive change within this world. It's appropriate they named me Hope. It ended up being the only hope they ever truly gave me.

I WANT A GLASS OF WATER

Have you ever encountered a child that did not speak? It could be unnerving as a parent. I myself did not have any children that did not want to forge communication with me as very young humans. I always thought of it as a bonding period between babies and their parents. Occasionally, there are those moments where you discover your baby has the inability to talk traditionally for one reason or another, and for that you find other ways of communicating, to form those bonds. There are so many ways for babies to hear or understand they recognize you as their parent, to know how you feel about them, or to see if they are the center of your universe as a parent. Young humans cannot grasp the totality of your love as a parent, but most times they can feel it, and that keeps them striving to learn communication with their parents. It's a most basic principle of family; the ability to communicate and show love or a lack thereof.

I was approaching the age of two and had not said a word. For all accounts I was a healthy baby. There was nothing that seemed to be ailing me in a way that would prohibit my ability to communicate, and yet Mother said I had not uttered a single word. I don't recall this period of time (obvious, but there you go), but Mother said she was continuously frustrated that I did not speak. She said she would bang pots and pans together to scare me to speak, jump, or cry, to confirm I was not deaf. This went on to the point where I became unresponsive to even that, so she took me to the doctor.

A doctor exam yielded that I was in fact a healthy baby. There was nothing developmentally wrong with me, and my hearing was sound. The doctor asked Mother what I did when I wanted something. As a near two-year-old, I had active desires and Mother said I would point to what I wanted. The doctor scolded her, telling her she needed to have me voice what it was that I wanted. He cautioned her that it didn't need to be perfectly formulated, but some effort at communication needed to happen.

Mother was frustrated at the scolding, and the fact that I could have been talking for months now. She ushered me home and commenced upon making me talk. We were in the kitchen, with her scolding me for banging on the pots and pans, becoming more and more frustrated because, according to her, I would just look at her and bang them together again (hopefully the irony is not lost here). She said I stood up, pointed to the sink, and started whining. She asked repeatedly what I wanted. I grunted, pointed, and cried for minutes, but Mother stood strong, even going to the other room so I could figure it out, or to get away from me, but I digress. According to her, after a while I walked up to her in the living room, looked at her and said, "I want a glass of water," like I had been talking for years. She obliged me and my silence was broken.

The silence was gone, but that was our first verbal communication. I have thought about this throughout my life, wondering if this played a part in formulating our relationship. My first words were not the mama, papa type of communication that forges those bonds of love. Rather mine were, from the start, frankly words of survival. We did not have a love bond in that moment, and I think my mother resented the fact that my response to her was not one of love, but one of necessity. I believe my mother has resented me for my entire existence, and that moment was among the many events that she used to break even further away from me.

Unknowingly, I spent decades trying to repair that moment. I didn't realize that it was one of the first slices into the fabric of our relationship that would ultimately cause our demise. I spent years of voicing, "I love you," "You're so pretty Mama", and "Do you love me, Mama?" all in an attempt to fix what was already mortally wounded. Mother often made no effort to hide her annoyance at my comments and questions. I vividly recall her more than once saying she didn't believe that I loved her. Even at such a young age I felt crushed by her words. It's no wonder I rarely felt her love. Hers was a love that was just not available to me. My relationship with her was one of necessity. It wasn't until adulthood that I realized I had been trying to fix something from the time I was a baby, something that was not my fault. Something that from such a young age I recognized as a need for survival.

Hope Doran

FLUSH!

Usually, as parents we find great delight in the smallest, let's just be honest, grossest things that our children do. They are either moments encapsulated by entertainment, milestones, or just the most basic of necessities. One would think the discovery of a very young child learning to go potty in the toilet would be a joyous occasion. Unfortunately, that was not the case for me. This is another story that is partial recollection and partial information given by Mother.

There it was, a shit in the toilet! Oh, how exciting!! Yeah, no. I recall hearing my mother yelling at me from the bathroom. I had been potty trained for a while at that point. I was still quite young, but despite my lack of years, I knew the tone in Mother's voice. I went into the bathroom, and she proceeded to yell at me because I did not flush the toilet. I told her I didn't use the potty because I didn't need to poo. She yelled at me, telling me not to lie, this escalated to the point where I was spanked, and sent to my bedroom.

A few days later it happened again! Through a tear-stained face, I told my mother I did not use the bathroom, but her rage over what she perceived as a lie was no match for my earnest face, and I got spanked again. She came into the room and told me I had to stay there until I told her the truth. I recall taking a tone with her that I immediately regretted, telling her I was not lying, and if I told her I did it, *that* would be the lie. She left the room enraged.

It was weeks before it was discovered that the cat we owned had actually taken a liking to using the toilet and begun using it as her litter box. Mother finally started to put the toilet seat down to keep the cat from shitting there. To this day, she tells the story like it's some funny lighthearted banter, leaving out the multiple times she disciplined me for something I didn't do.

She never did apologize for that. Even if she had, the damage was done. It was traumatizing for me to use the bathroom especially to poop, so oftentimes I wouldn't. When I did, I would be sure to let Mother know I had, and that I also flushed. Sometimes I pooped in my room because she had started locking the door to my room at night. I pooped in the corner of my bedroom and cleaned it up before she found it. Always making sure to flush.

LOCKED IN

Mother instituted the locking of the bedroom at night. I was solidly 3 years old when this occurred. She claimed it was supposed to be a safety measure. Mother never missed a moment to tell me how unruly I was as a child. She told me that because I did not like to do as I was told, she would help secure my safety by locking my door. However, that did not deafen my ears to the front door closing as my parents went out to do whatever they left to do late into the evening. With their exit, I would often try the door, but it would consistently be locked.

I recall being incredibly scared and would wait up listening for their return. Oftentimes I would fall into fitful sleep while waiting for the sound of the front door. I would later be awakened by their whispered voices from beyond the door as they readied themselves for bed. I was in my room, scared to be alone but according to Mother, safe. At some point during my lockdowns, the terrors started.

I hated being locked in. Not so much for the loss of freedom, I was 3 for Christ's sake. There was a fear attached to the confinement that I struggled with. I suffered waves of panic every night although I was too young to realize it for what it was. It felt like a heaviness that surrounded me, clutching me from the inside. It was a feeling that I found no escape from. I grew to hate the evening hours, which didn't help my plight with regards to Mother.

I recognized that I would often push Mother's boundaries when I was young, but not anymore than most other children. I rebelled against being locked in, which for Mother only fueled her desire to entrap me. My fear left me exhausted, and I would often fall into fitful sleep. I recall waking up in the middle of the night to see tiny people in my room. The bedroom floor was littered with them. I sat in my bed peering over the edge, watching them as they frantically tried to get out of the room. I could hear their screaming, crying, and fighting over one another to escape. There was one point where I watched them as they attempted to light the door on fire. That was the first time I thought they were there perhaps trying to help me. As weird as all of this sounds, the next morning there was a small scorch mark at the bottom of the door. I never understood what happened or what exactly they were trying to accomplish, but after that night they never showed up again.

I wish that was the end of my experience, but it wasn't. Other strange and scary occurrences began happening. There were nights when the walls would transform into these massive trees that engulfed the room. The new, eerie forest would have people searching for me within its darkened web of branches holding deep green shades of foliage. I would hide under my covers wishing them away, but when I came out for air, it was all still there, they were still there. I would often see the two children looking for me. It was a boy and a girl. They looked hollow and sad as they would walk over to the side of my bed and stare at me in silence as I shook in uncontrollable fear. What I was seeing and feeling was so real to me. Even as I write it, I recall my fear. I remember being terrified and panicking, trying to get out of my locked bedroom, unsuccessfully. I pounded on the door, but it echoed into an empty apartment.

Unfortunately, with the transition I was so scared I got sick and defecated in my room to the point where there was no hiding it. The next day Mother was furious, but I told her I was locked in, and they weren't there to let me out. The lock came off the door that day, but my terror over the room did not. Mother got me a Jesus poster and night-light to help soothe me, but my room still haunted me with the same strange, terrifying things. I hid the poster and night-light away, and the terrors finally stopped.

Years later I told my mother this story. She told me there were people that lived below us that practiced witchcraft. I often wonder how she knew that. I also wonder why she was okay with leaving me alone, locked up knowing that. I also consider that her story is complete bullshit, and something she said to separate herself from the trauma she caused me. I don't know if all the events in my bedroom were actually seen, or if my brain was trying to manage the trauma of the locked door. I do know that to this day, I don't like to be confined behind a closed door. I always prefer to have some visual form of power that offers an ability to escape, even if I know I am perfectly safe.

Hope Doran

POOL TIME

From the youngest of ages, I was awkward. I never had a strong sense of self as a child. So, friends that came through were few and far between. When I had them, I'm sure I held on too tight. I recall moments of lost friendships as a result of my insecurities. I feel I was looking for the love and acceptance that was not available from my mother. It made things awkward in friendships.

My mother had gained a neighbor friend in one of the many moves we made in my younger years. They lived in a house neighboring our apartment complex. That came with the neighbor's daughter, who was my age. We got along well, and I had what I recall as my first friendship.

She was turning 4 and having a birthday party. I was ecstatic over the idea of being able to go. It was to be my first birthday party I recall attending. She, having siblings who had friends was having a large party. It also was a pool party, so all of us kids were out back for a while. I did not know how to interact with so many kids. As a result, my mood shifted during her party. When I initially got there, I was entranced, but as the party progressed, I became awkward and sullen. I remember feeling jealous that I didn't have all my friend's time and made a scene in the pool. Rather than helping me process and using it as a learning moment, Mother ushered me home, irritated that my attitude forced her to leave the adult part of the party early. I was sent to my room sad and angry.

After that, things returned to normal and seemed fine for a time. My friend and I reengaged, and I felt safe having her to myself again. My mother and the neighbor would chat and us girls would be outside playing in the pool or wrestling around in the backyard. I don't remember much, but it was fun to have a friend, and we both enjoyed each other's company. I feel that she was a kindred spirit. She was another outcast of sorts, just trying to survive the poverty stereotypes and meanness that were already showing their ugly heads in our lives.

But then, without warning we stopped going over. I never understood why. Mother told me she saw us in the small pool "being inappropriate." I didn't understand what she meant. Later, I came across an old photo of my friend and I hugging in the pool. She snatched the photo from my little fingers and walked off. I didn't know what it meant to be gay then, but as an adult, I've often wondered if Mother saw signs of the inevitable in me. She never did tell me what she saw or what happened. All I remember was a friendship lost.

I SWEAR

A lot of things happened during this same period as the loss of the first friend I remember. We lived in an apartment, on the outskirts of an impoverished area of Illinois. Mother was full of spit and vinegar, and seemingly never skipped a beat to use me as a way of release. It made me scared of her. This fear was clouded by my massive desire to feel love from her. It left me in a very strange place of disconnects and rage for a child so young. It was in this apartment that I truly felt lost emotionally. Of course, I didn't know that at the time. At the time I only recall having massive amounts of anger and sadness. As a small child, I did not recognize what it was or how to handle or heal my scared little heart and mind.

Mother would often send me out to play during the day. It was back in the 'come back at dusk era,' so no harm there. The harm came when I would play with the other kids in the neighborhood. Most of them were Italian, and did not speak much, if any English. But what they did know in English were curse words, to which I was introduced, along with vernaculars of their own. I would come home from my fun days with them spewing every curse word in the book. I thought it was funny, because that's what the neighbor kids were doing, and we all thought it was humorous. We all laughed as they listened to the foul words roll off my tongue. Mother did not find my newfound vocabulary so funny, and I got my mouth washed out with soap.

Time after time this happened to the point, I actually had a preference of the soap I wanted her to use on me. The moment I expressed my preference was the first moment I saw my mother stammer. I still can recall the look of rage on her face when I asked for Palmolive soap instead of the coarse, granulated Lava soap she came at me with in that moment. Attached to that look was also shock and irritation.

She spun on her heels and retreated into the kitchen. She returned shortly with the plastic container of Palmolive soap. I watched as she came at me, the green soapy liquid sloshing around in its container, waiting to be released into my filthy mouth. She grabbed my head and proceeded to cleanse my mouth of foul language through the power of Palmolive soap.

For the life of me I don't understand how I did not drown in soap that day. The thick liquid ran down my face and throat as I choked and gasped for air. All the while, my head locked in her clutches. I gurgled in her grasp until she was satisfied that she had cleansed me of my wicked ways, if only for the moment. She released me from her clutches with a slight shove. I tried not to vomit, knowing it would be something I would have to clean up as part of my discipline. I never wanted Palmolive soap again, but that was okay, she resumed her discipline work with the belt after that.

MATCHES

At some point, the parental units must have been doing better for work. We moved onto a lovely log cabin in what I suspect was an unincorporated area of Illinois. The tiny home was nestled into a rolling hillside that offered space for me to wander around. I often welcomed the quiet isolating space. It enveloped me in comfort as I sat and watched the tall grass dance around aimlessly in the breeze. I welcomed the escape to fresh air from the smoke-filled house.

Mother was a heavy smoker when I was young. It was the thing to do back then. No judgment to any smokers out there, including her. I would watch her light up cigarette after cigarette from a white and red box. First smacking it against the box before sliding it between her thin lips and lighting it. I observed her as she inhaled deeply the vapors it rendered. Even from a very young age I recall the soothing effect it had on her, and I was intrigued. I would sit, hidden away in the corner of the room, watching her smoke. She would breathe in, holding the moment like a warm embrace before beginning her slow exhale filling her space in a dreamlike state of repurposed air in the form of smoke, which covered her like a thick blanket. Her eyes were sometimes closed, deepening her experience. I did not know this at the time, but for her, it was ritualistic.

My desire for her acceptance perked over this habit. She told me on numerous occasions that I was not to play with her things, especially her cigarettes. My wanting to be like her plagued me. Even at that age I saw mirroring as a way to garner acceptance, and that was something I desperately wanted from her. Despite her blatant warning to leave them be, her cigarettes called to me as a way to connect to her. I watched her, how her fingers moved, caressing the sticks. I watched her extract one from its box, letting the cigarette rest between her lips as she struck the match, willing one to come to life. Once lit, searing it to the cigarette, waiting for it to bring her peace. It was her version of sage for protection. In hindsight it was likely mine.

I embraced her ritual, learned from it. I watched carefully, her process, how she breathed, how far she would take the cigarette down before she would smoosh its life out into one of the numerous ashtrays that lived in our house. I recall thinking in my 4 or 5-year-old brain that I'd been fully trained, simply by observing Mother, and that I was ready.

I had hidden a few cigarettes away in my room, along with a book of matches and an ashtray. They had gone undetected, and I recall being relieved. Mother had a horse back then, and she was out with Commander on a ride. I sat on my bed, which was adorned with a yellow Raggedy Ann comforter looking at my prizes. I was excited, and my heart was pounding.

I pulled a cigarette out of the collection, rolling it around with my thumb and forefinger, trying to envision how Mother would prep herself, recalling that she would do this before switching to the fore and middle finger for lighting. I first tapped the cigarette against the box I had retrieved from the trash, then raised the cigarette up to my mouth, breathing in the heavy tobacco smell, which permeated from the white stick as it rested on my young lips.

My excitement quickly waned as I attempted to light the first match. It seemed so easy in my mother's trained hands, but in mine they faltered. Match after match was bent, ripped, and destroyed without the flame of life as I attempted to strike it. My failed attempts littered the floor and my bed.

As I was working on a new match, I smelled something. I looked past the match in my hand to see that one of my previous attempts had smoldered to life. My yellow comforter had a burn hole. I snuffed it out with my hand, burning my palm in the process. The comforter was burnt in the center, towards the edge of the bed. Excitement quickly turned to dread. Even in my young brain, I knew there was no hiding the scorch mark. I knew I was in trouble. I could already feel the burning sear of the belt across my backside. I put everything back in their original places and waited.

My wait was not long. Mother came back a couple of hours later and I was in my room, nervously pretending to play with toys. Despite the lapse of time, there was no escaping the smell of burnt polyester, which was still heavy in the air along with the sulfuric smell from the matches. Mother eyed the room suspiciously and I waited, squishing the blister that had formed on my hand. Her eyes came to rest as the deep brown burn on the comforter caught her attention. She eyed me and asked what happened. I don't recall what I said, but it was a lie. It's the first lie I recall telling. She saw me pushing on my hand and without asking, snatched it up for closer viewing. She looked at it, then at me, dropping my hand from her grasp. My hand fell to my side as if it was lead. She left the room without another word.

I could hear her stomping around the house. This was a departure from her usual steps to spanking me with her hand or worse, with a belt. My childish mind grew curious. Perhaps it wouldn't be as bad as I thought it would be. I sat on the bed and waited in the now silence that rang through the house. It was a while before she returned, snatching my burnt hand up in hers, yanking me out of my room to the bathroom.

Once there, I stood still as she yelled at me. I don't recall much of what she was yelling, other than saying if I liked lighting matches so much, she would help me with that. She then shoved a book of matches in my hand and ushered me in front of the sink. I stared at the sink confused. It was filled with water. Surrounding the sink were numerous books of matches. "They're all for you," she stated. "You're going to light every single one of these. Maybe then you'll listen to me when I tell you to stay out of my things." Part of me was relieved. She didn't know about the cigarettes. Nevertheless, I was terrified by the look on her face. "GO," she yelled, so I did.

I don't know how long I was there, or how many

matchbooks there were. I do know I had at least attempted to strike each and every one. I do know when all was said and done my fingers were blistered and burned. My cries of apology fell to deaf ears as she sat silent and watched me strike every single match. Her eyes were cold, and mouth pursed as she watched. When I finally finished, she stood up, looked at the mess, told me to clean it up and never touch her things again. She never looked at the hands I complained about for days. I never touched her ritual again. It came with a fury I was unable to match.

Hope Doran

ADRENALINE RUSH

Most of us have very definitive moments that we know beyond a shadow of a doubt shape us. They are usually impactful tales that can be funny, adventurous, harrowing, or tragic. I have never met a person that remembered their first adrenaline rush.

I do.

I was quite young, perhaps 5. I was at my grandmother's house. I recall it being a favorite place to go. It had a porch swing that, when you swung hard, lifted you past the deck to view the rocky ground below. It was a lot of fun, but I was constantly being scolded by Mother to not swing so hard. In spite of that, when she wasn't around, I would launch myself out from the deck again. Oftentimes Mother would sit on the deck as well and when she did, I found it quite soothing swaying gently in the summer air, pretending as if she wasn't there and the wind would whisk me away at any moment to something better.

The front porch was massive to my young years, and I enjoyed playing on it. From the deck, through the front door the smell of grandma's house filled my head with warm feelings of comfort. It is one I still catch from time to time. It had an old, well-worn smell to it. One of those smells that tell you there's been love in it. It had a slight musty smell, combined with the smell of life, the love of cooking, the pride of cleaning and the feeling of calmness in just being present. Very rarely do I come across this smell, but when I do, it's like I'm back with my grandmother, watching her cook, taking her fresh cooked goods to the porch to swing and play on the deck.

The house was on the small side, and the attic had been converted to a bedroom, which is where we stayed when we visited. The staircase leading to it was off the kitchen, in an 'L' shape, with three steps going up before making a left and advancing up the main part of the staircase. It was a small space, but served its purpose and is part of the few fond memories I have in childhood.

On one of the rare visits there, my folks were gone, and I was left with grandma. I had gone from playing in the house, to the deck, then out in the fields surrounding the house. I was bored. I wanted more. My restless mind wandered as I kicked the dirt making my way back to the porch. Then I spied my Big Wheel, and a plan began formulating in my young mind.

Getting the Big Wheel into the house was easy enough. Grandma was busy doing other things. However, getting it up the stairs was another story. My small body was not well versed in dragging such bulky things up anything, let alone a narrow staircase.

My resilience paid off, and I reached the top and entered the room. I quickly spun the Big Wheel around, facing it down the stairs. I sat on it contemplating the possibility. With doubt in my mind, I got off and headed down the stairs. I got to the first landing, looking down at the turn I would have to make to complete the last three stairs and zoom off through the kitchen. Confident I could do it, I returned upstairs.

I slid into the seat of the Big Wheel, my heart pounding. I looked down the staircase that once again scoffed at me, telling me I wouldn't be able to do it. I pushed the thought back, leaning back into the seat, letting it hug my back as I rocked back, then fourth, back, and fourth, the heels of my shoes lingering on the edge of the first step in my descent. My heart was pounding in my throat, coursing blood through my body in waves. The palms of my hands were clammy as I tightly gripped the handlebars.

It happened so quickly, the shift from no to yes. There was something deep inside me that screamed do it, so I did. The heels of my feet pushed off that first step and I flew down the stairs, each one taking a piece of me. I didn't care. Each stair I made it past was a victory. I clamored down that staircase like a locomotive, my screeches of delight the horn! The bottom was coming fast, and in spite of my plan to lean hard to the right and force the turn that would launch me to success, I slammed hard into the wall. The force of the collision turned me into temporary wallpaper before I slumped down and came to rest on the floor.

My grandmother rushed in to see what the commotion was. I was like a rag doll on the floor. I could see her processing what had just happened. Once she knew I was alright, her gaze shifted to the wall. I didn't realize it, but my adventure had put a hole in the wall. I started to cry. I told her I was sorry and ran up to the attic to await the return of my parental units.

I was sobbing on the bed when grandma came up the

stairs. She sat with me until I stopped crying. She said everything was fine and I had nothing to worry about. I told her I would be in trouble, but she consoled me telling me not to say anything about it and she wouldn't mention the event. It was the first time I put my faith in someone, and she did not let me down. Mother never found out from her.

It wasn't until I was into my adulthood that I realized my grandmother had not only protected me but protected herself as well. I casually told my mother the story (leaving out the bond of silence). I always knew things were not good between my mother and grandmother, but I hadn't thought about Mother's reaction to the event as it pertained to my grandmother. Mother tried to play it off, but I saw the slightest flicker of fire in her eyes as she said "Hm, she never told us about that." In that moment, I realized that grandma had known how things were for me, and her silence was one small gift she could give me. It was a cherished gift, even if I didn't realize what it was at the time.

WHERE'S HOPE?

When people move, they usually have the thought that they are safe. Back when I was young, there was no such thing as internet or cell phones for a quick search to help ensure there were no unsavory individuals, or people with a police record living in your new neighborhood. It was a fly by the seat of your pants world, where a simple smile was gold, and if you were quiet, you were considered safe.

It was yet another move for us. To be fair, it was to be my favorite home in Illinois before everything that happened there. It was a sleepy residential area with open backyards, family homes, and trees in yards that provided for lazy summer days, the raking of leaves in the fall, and snowy frigid winters. My favorite memory there was our last winter at the house. We had a snowstorm, and the snow piled up so high I made a slide down the side of the house. For all other seasons, there was a park down the street that I would walk or bike to and spend most days that weren't involved with other goings on.

Still awkward in my young childhood, my friend list was minimal. Once again, my mother filled that void, having befriended a woman with two young boys. We spent days together tooling around the neighborhood and hanging out in the backyard. By all accounts, we got along well. I was a tomboy, so we soon developed a friendship greater than the one of necessity. I remember being grateful for that.

The day I was abducted is not completely clear in my mind. They say trauma lends itself to blocking things or events out of memory to protect the human. I did not recall the abduction for years, and the recollection of it seemed both foggy and abrupt. Like a knowledge that events occurred, peppered with certain parts of recollection, but with a knowing that there is so, so much more. The pieces are incomplete, but the recollections I have are palpable. As a human that endured such terror, I will recount it as best I can.

It had been a fun day with my two friends. We were all similar in age, between 5 and 7 years old. We had spent the day playing in the house and out in the expansive backyard. After tiring of that, we took to the sidewalk and went to the park. It was a sunny day, and I recall staying at the park for a good clip of time before we got hungry and started our way back home. We were walking slowly, engrossed in childish humor. I recall the lighthearted feeling of sharing a moment with friends.

We passed an individual that had his arm in a sling, walking with a paper bag full of groceries. As we passed, he fumbled the bag with his one good arm, and failing miserably, the bag hit the ground. The contents splayed out onto the sidewalk. I hesitated as I watched him stoop down, attempting to pick up his items with his one unbound hand. He viewed me watching and asked for assistance. I looked at my two friends, who had continued walking, and recall thinking I could catch up to them, so I walked to the man and began helping him reload his goods.

As I hurriedly helped the man, I felt uncomfortable. I hollered out to my friends, but they were too far away and did not hear me. The man stood and I handed him the bag and stepped towards my friends in a nervous retreat. As I began to turn away from the man, he fumbled the bag again and it tore. I caught the bag and handed it back to him. The man asked me to help him to his house. He said it was just a few houses down as he pointed to an unknown house in the direction of my friends. He said it was on my way anyways, so it would not be too much for me to help. I saw that he was right and saw no way out of assisting him. With his first victory, the man handed me his bag and we started down the sidewalk.

He attempted to make small talk with me as we strode along, but my eyes were fixed on the sidewalk ahead, where I could no longer see my friends. I remember feeling uncomfortable, uneasy, and wishing I had just continued with them and never engaged in this act of helpfulness. My body was sweaty with an unfamiliar dread, and my hands began trembling. I felt trapped.

It's interesting how your subconscious knows your situation before your consciousness picks it up. Despite my spotty recollection of all the events, this lesson is one I have never let go of. When the hairs on the back of my neck rise like they did that day, I know what that is. I always listen to that same sixth sense that I felt that day but was too young to recognize it for the warning it was.

We made the left turn into his driveway and walked up towards the house. My feet were dragging, and I sensed a shift in the man from friendly to stern. I was well versed in stern attitudes from my mother and wanted to get away. I attempted to hand the man his bag, but he refused to take it. He said he needed help with the front door, as he was unable to retrieve his keys from the pocket of his jeans. It was at that point he grabbed the bag to free my hands.

I was too young to catch what was unfolding before me. You see, his right arm was the one that was in the sling, but he said his keys were in his right pocket. If his arm were truly wounded, the keys would have been elsewhere. Nevertheless, he presented his pocket to me and demanded I retrieve the keys and open the door. The niceties were gone, and I was in panic mode.

My hand reluctantly entered the top of his pocket. I was not able to reach all the way down and quickly withdrew my hand and said I couldn't reach them, He insisted, saying he would not be able to get into the house, and I had been so helpful to this point I should just help him with his keys. He squatted down ever so slightly so I could reach further in. I could feel his breath hot, shallow, and controlled, on the top of my head.

My hesitant young fingers reached in with his prodding to go deeper down into his pocket. I obliged, and dug deeper, finding nothing except what I now know was his erect penis. There were no keys. I began to retract my hand, my cheeks ablaze with unknown shame. The man scolded me, telling me they were in there, demanding I retrace my way back down his pocket of dread. As I was shifting to run, the man laughed it off, smiling as he said the keys were in his other pocket. Before I could register what was happening, he sprung into motion. In one swift move he unlocked the door. I recall him throwing the groceries into the house and grabbing me. That is all that my mind has processed.

Years would pass before I recalled these events, and more years before I would talk to my mother about it. It was during a period of time when, as a young adult, I would often go to my parent's house. I had a particularly rough night full of nightmares. I don't typically recall my dreams, so when I do, I tend to pay attention. This particular dream felt like an out of body experience. I was watching the events, but also knew it was me I was watching. I was splayed out on a kitchen table with a man in between my legs. I was watching from behind, so I never saw his face, but his hair was shaggy and unruly. Then I recalled being tossed into a closet, being told to be quiet, and I woke up.

Mother asked me why I was so tired, and I regaled her with my dream. When I finished, I offhandedly said something about feeling like it was related to my abduction. Mother's face lost all color, and she responded with "you remember that? What exactly do you remember? When did you recall this?" I could hear the panic in her questions. I proceeded with telling her what I recalled and saw her shudder in disbelief. I didn't think about it until that moment, but Mother never told me about the abduction. She asked me several times if that was all I remembered before offering me her version of events.

Mother said the two boys had returned to the house and

were playing out back. She said she didn't give it much thought until she went outside sometime later but did not see me. She said she asked the boys where I was, and they told her I had stopped to help a man with groceries. She said she thought this was strange and asked the boys to show her the house.

As I write this, I realize the boys did not know where I was. They were out of my sight by the time I got to the man's house. But Mother said she went with the boys to the house and knocked on the door. A man answered, and Mother said she told him she wanted her daughter. The man denied any knowledge of me. According to my mother, the boys confirmed it was the same man, but again the man denied my existence and closed the door on her.

Mother said she banged on the door again and the man angrily answered, leaving just enough room in the doorway to converse. He told her to leave him alone and not come back. She said he told her he did not have her kid and slammed the door on her one last time. Mother said she had a feeling that she needed to intervene immediately, and grabbed a chair on the porch, raising it over her head to throw it through the front window. Before she could follow through with the throw, the man opened the door and gave me back to her and she took me home.

That was it. End of story...at least hers.

I cannot begin to explain how many ways this story makes no sense at all. Mother offered no further information, and in hindsight, I wish I had pushed harder for it. Once her words were spoken, it's as if a wall went up.

We never spoke of it again. I assume that's because she did not tell me the truth and would be unable to keep her story straight.

I get the sense that there was psychological therapy involved for me following the event, but nothing I can firmly recall. I feel that it was a therapy that involved burying trauma as a way of dealing with it. I believe that happened because Mother's story does not add up. Additionally, I get sensations of therapy events that lend themselves to that type of process. Mother never mentioned any kind of therapy. She didn't say she took me to a medical doctor. She never mentioned filing a report with the police. She never said she was sorry for the things that did, or may have happened, or even apologized for the event happening and the subsequent trauma it caused. It was like the event was closed to her, and I didn't matter.

It enrages me that Mother made herself out to be the hero. Deep down, I doubt she really was. I don't know with certainty how I was recovered, or what was done to me, during or after the incident. All I know is that it did in fact happen. I think Mother made a concerted effort to bury the trauma deep in the recesses of my young mind thinking it would never again rise to the surface and deface her.

I often wonder what happened to that man. More so I fear what was done to other young children because of my parental units' silence on the entire matter. It haunts me. Sometimes I wonder if it ever haunted the parental units. Did they even give it a thought? Did they wonder if horrible things happened to other children? If so, have their choices haunted them? Did they ponder what the traumatic event really did to me emotionally, physically, and spiritually? Did they ever care about me in that context at all?

The parental units moved us out to California after that. The reason for the move? According to Mother, after the door handle to the car broke off in her hand in the cruel Illinois winter, she told Father she was moving to a place where it never snowed, and he was welcome to join her if he wanted. I ponder the truthfulness to that as well. It makes me wonder who, or what they were hiding or why we were really running. Regardless, that was the end of Illinois. I have never been back.

GRANDMA

Our travels out to California were eventful. Most everything had been sold, save what we could fit into a tired avocado green Pinto car and a new tan Chevy van. We moved with a bird and two cats, sleeping on a mattress in the back of the van. I remember being excited about the adventure, having heard my parental units discussing the places we would visit in our travels to the Golden State. The biggest excitement was the destination. My beloved grandmother had moved to California, and we would be staying at her new home while we established ourselves in California. I was elated.

Quite quickly the novelty of travel wore off for me. I can assure you I was not the best travel companion. I began to riddle the parental units with questions about how much longer, when was the next stop, when were we going to eat, and why was it taking so long?? I'm quite certain I drove them to the brink of insanity as they were driving us to California.

One of the most memorable of events for me was the time we were in a restaurant and my mother's purse was stolen off the back of her chair. The parental units quickly discovered the loss, as well as who took the bag. They hurriedly paid the bill and ran out the door with me in tow. We jumped into the van and began our pursuit of the thieves.

I remember following the thieves around by car for a period of time before they threw the purse out over a bridge. We watched as the colorful, decorative, embroidered bag landed with a splash into the waters below, engulfing its brown leather in its watery grasp. At that point we stopped. The parental units had lost. It was not just the purse itself, but half of their funds for the drive out to California, as well as Mother's ID, and other important paperwork. It was a big blow for them.

Shortly after that, the Pinto stopped working. After a surmise of the vehicle, it was determined that it needed to be junked. We crammed what we had from the Pinto into the van and continued on. My biggest disappointment was that we were all now traveling in the same vehicle. With my slight refuge in traveling alone with my father now gone, I became more sullen as we trucked on in our journey.

Other eventful moments I recall were the KOA campsites, the Bad Lands, the Grand Canyon, and Mount Rushmore. All of those things had an impact on me. Even at such a young age I recognized the beauty of the national parks, and their importance in nature. At one point Mother was upset because I was what she called 'restless' while at Mount Rushmore. She yanked on my arm pulling me so close to her I could see the pores on her face. Her hot breath landed on my face as she told me I needed to appreciate what I was seeing because I would likely never see it again. My arm hurt from the pressure of her fingers around it. I settled in and was quiet, tears burning my face as the red marks appeared on my upper arm after her release.

What she did not realize was that she stole the moment from me. Rather than let me enjoy it as a nearly 8-year-old child, which I had been doing, she reprimanded me and insisted I view it from her perspective. Her narrow-minded way of thinking also included a passive aggressive comment that it would not be seen by me again, so I better enjoy it. Of course, in her narrative this was all at her expense. That is something narcissists and mentally unstable individuals do. They force their narrative onto you so they feel better about themselves, often ruining the moment, event, or relationship that you may have as an individual separate from them.

We could not get to grandma's house soon enough. When we finally did, I leapt out of the van and into her eager arms. Mother and Father exited the van and melted into the still hot Central Valley evening air. They unloaded essentials and we went in for the night. Grandmother had created another comfortable home filled with love. She had a sewing room as well as a guest room. I stayed in the sewing room and as I readied for bed, pondered all the things Grandma would create in the space as I slipped off to sleep.

From my perspective, for the briefest of moments, things were fantastic. Father was looking for work and Mother and I would stay at Grandma's house. As time went on though, I could sense the tension between Mother and Grandma. I was too young to understand, but I felt it. As a reprieve, Grandma would let me play dress up in her room. Nothing was off limits, and I would spend hours in her space. She even let me fish for crawdads in her backyard creek, all dressed up. Sometimes I was in some of her nicest clothes. I felt like I mattered there under her attentive eyes.

As the weeks progressed Mother was becoming increasingly irritable. She became someone to avoid at all costs. Apparently, the same held true with Grandma, so Mother started taking me out with her to get out of the house. It was always blisteringly hot as it was midsummer, and I resented her taking me away from the coolness of Grandma's house.

On one of our outings, we went with Father to Bakersfield for a work interview. It was incredibly hot, but we did not have the money to go into one of the many restaurants, so for a while, we sat in the van. I recall hoping Father got the job so we would be closer to Grandma. It helped me endure the sweltering temperatures of the van while Mother went to look for water. Mother returned sometime later with Father, with a small cup of water. They were in a heated discussion as they approached the van. Mother was flailing her arms this way and that, in what appeared to be protest as her mouth tightened as it so often did when she was in a rage. Father shrugged his shoulders and Mother's arms went flying towards the heavens, spilling the water. She looked irritatingly at the cup before opening the van door and handing me a mostly empty cup. My parched mouth guzzled the remaining liquid and I settled into the seat. We all sat in silence on the ride back. Mother spent most of the ride glaring at Father.

Father did not get the job. Mother sought out ways to distance us from Grandma. She posted an ad in a small-town newspaper looking for housing. She got a response, and we ended up moving to the Santa Cruz Mountains. Before we left, I had heard several arguments between the three of them. Most of the arguments were in hushed cutting tones that I was not able to discern, save the heated results. During one of these many verbal altercations Mother broke her whispered tongue lashing and loudly made mention of blood being thicker than water, to which Grandma scoffed at her, and made a comment under her breath before she walked off.

I asked Mother what she meant by the comment. She told me it was something Grandma had said to her while playing a card game with Father's side of the family. According to Mother, it was a game where an individual had opportunities to "burn" other players. Mother said Grandma had the chance to "burn" my aunt, or my mother. She chose my mother stating as she did "Well honey, blood's thicker than water."

The funny thing is the comment, which was meant to cut so deep, was misused. Loosely translated, the bloodshed from shared battles is a stronger tie than the water that holds a baby within the womb. It's an interesting irony considering the battles the two of them engaged in. Regardless of the misuse, it was taken as such, so a misused quote turned a relationship sour.

That would be a thread that my mother chose to stitch through her entire relationship with my grandmother. Mother never forgave her for the comment as she received it, and Grandma never cared enough to talk to Mother about it. As stated earlier, I think she saw my mother for what she truly was, so she did not care if the comment cut. I also wonder if Grandma knew some of the details surrounding my abduction. I never thought to ask her later in life.

Regardless, I cared that the comment was made. That comment cost me time with my grandmother. I suspect if it wasn't that comment, it would have been something else. Grandma obviously did not fit well into my mother's narrative.

WHO'S IMPORTANT?

We settled into our new, expansive home in the isolated mountains of Santa Cruz. Although it was big, it was a very, very tired house that had long since passed its hay-day. To say we were poor would be highly accurate. Father had finally gained employment at a mom-and-pop electronic repair place in town, and so began our new life. Mother was feeling fortunate in her ad for housing. We got lucky, having a wealthy family offer the guest home on their winery property for well below market value for renting.

I was excited by the wide-open space of the 10 acres we got to call home. I explored all its nooks and crannies, coming across adventurous finds such as wooded hiking trails created by the animals in the area, or an abandoned smoke house carved into a rock. Next to that was a ridiculously large oak tree that I felt a bond to. I would terrify my mother by climbing high within its many perches, gleeful in her response and inability to readily yank me down. I would settle into the recesses of its expansive branches, filled with prickly leaves. They covered me like a warm blanket, keeping me safe, if only for a moment.

The beauty of the area was dampened by the start of school, which was nestled into the mountains a mile from our home. That meant I could walk to school. The school was filled with wealth, and my young mind dove back into familiar territory. Very quickly I realized I did not fit into what seemed to be the social norms of the area. I wore the wrong clothes, was unruly, tomboyish, heavyset, and came to school with a scantily filled brown lunch bag. My social counterparts all had their Esprit attire, or other name brand clothes, perfectly styled hair, and tossed around their expensive fancy lunch boxes as though they were a paper sack. I was crushed, once again realizing I was an outcast. I took my position as proudly as I could, slipping all too easily into my familiar place within school society. Almost instantly upon my arrival into third grade I was defeated and broken inside as the taunting and ridicule towards me began, for a life that was not of my making.

I continued on in that state, seeking out what little joys I could find. My favorite time in school was time set aside for art. One of the projects was to draw our family portrait. I was very excited for this project, and the crayons took on a life of their own as I put my family to paper for artistic display. I was proud of that drawing and turned it in with a smile on my face.

Quite soon I realized I had made a mistake. Not a mistake of wrongdoing, but rather a mistake of bearing my heart. My teacher had concerns with my portrait. She asked if my grandmother lived with us. I said "No, but we stayed with her over the summer." The teacher then asked me why I drew her in the household family, and I told her it was because I love her. The teacher accepted this, and I was excused.

I sauntered home, enjoying my favorite time, that of being alone. It was during my path to and from home and school that I dreamt of what-ifs and a future full of possibilities. It was in those moments that I was normal and created scenarios where I was loved, fit in, and had friends. It was in those times I dreamt of a place where I was worth something. I would wander around and find my way off the asphalt road into an apple orchard that was private property. It smelled glorious there. I could hear the bees buzzing in the branches, heavy laden with blossoms or fruit, depending on the season. If anyone saw me there, they thought nothing of it. My daydreams faded into the recesses of my mind as my destination came into view, but still, they survived, in spite of whatever the days or nights held for me.

I walked into the house and immediately felt that something was wrong. Mother came at me with her icy blue eyes that instantly had me on edge, quickly processing my day in an attempt to figure out what I had done wrong. I came up empty and stood in front of my mother as she demanded to know why she and Father were being called into the school for a parent teacher meeting. I assured her I did not know why, but my words fell on deaf ears as she informed me, we were all meeting at the school the following day.

The next day was a long one. I knew the meeting was at the end of the day, and I was anxious. Unable to focus, I asked my teacher why she had called the meeting. She assured me that I was not in trouble, and not to worry about it. I struggled to find faith in her words but was unsuccessful.

The passing of time to the end of the day may as well

have been an eternity. My breath came in nervous pulses as I walked to the office. I entered and the teacher was there, with the principal as well as my parents. I did not understand what all of this was for. I slumped into a chair and awaited to find what my wrongdoing was and its inevitable punishment to which I knew was coming once we returned to the walls of our home.

The teacher started out light enough. She regaled my parents with the polite niceties about having me in her class. Even in third grade, I knew it was bullshit. She concluded with discussing the family portrait project. She made a comment to the effect that in all her years of teaching she has never come across a family portrait such as this. With that, she presented my masterpiece. I was proud of that portrait of us. I didn't understand what was wrong.

I stared at my work confused, the parental units aghast as they took it in. There, in a brilliant red crayon was my grandmother, larger than life, practically filling half the paper. She was donned in one of the many outfits I wore over the summer. Next to her was myself, proudly holding her hand dressed in yellow crayon, also in one of her outfits. The parental units next to me were in dark blue crayon, drawn in stick form as opposed to the adornments grandma and myself wore. I could see the smoldering in Mother's eyes as the teacher proceeded with telling my parents this was not healthy. She went on to say that my perception of our family, specifically the obvious role my grandmother played in my life was not normal.

The teacher concluded with strongly recommending

counseling for me to correct my family views and align them with something more traditional. She again said this wasn't healthy. I could feel the tears of fear burning my cheeks as I listened to her repeat her earlier mantra of telling me I wasn't in trouble, whilst knowing full well the contained rage smoldering within my mother.

We left the office. The parental units chose to walk ahead of me in silence. They entered the car and told me to walk home. It was one of two times I walked home from school with no hope for the future. By the time I got home, they were sitting across from each other, and beckoned me to join them. They proceeded to tell me that time with grandma would be more limited. They told me I would be going to therapy. It ended up being the first therapy I recall going to. They sent me to my room, where I gladly retreated to its safety.

I don't remember much of the actual therapy, save one very specific memory. I had been seeing the therapist, who seemed to uncover a lot of pent-up rage I had towards Mother. They prescribed a therapy that involved a Nerf bat. I was allowed to hit whomever I wanted in the room, but I had to give a reason for the hit. I do recall hitting Father, but Mother gave me a look of challenge, which I gladly accepted under the "safety" of the therapist. I rattled off so many grievances and hit Mother so many times the therapist had to stop the session.

The therapist stated they had not encountered an occasion where the subject did not run out of reasons to swing the bat. The ride home was deafening in its silence.

For once I was not disciplined when I thought for sure I would be. I think the parental units were in shock. I stopped going to therapy shortly after. I can only assume they deemed me as cured.

BATHROOM TIME

Shortly following the end of my therapy, I became even more sullen in class. My teacher couldn't even find any niceties to lie about in speaking with Mother as they called one parent teacher conference after another. I stopped doing my homework and retreated to the corners of the school whenever I could. I began stealing from my fellow students in an attempt to gain some small piece of the worlds they lived in. That only led to more troubles with my fellow students, the staff, and the parental units. I was ashamed of who I was and would often sit in the corners and hide, wishing myself out of existence, but having no way of knowing how to escape.

I recall one time in particular when we were all sitting in class doing silent work. I had to go to the bathroom and raised my hand. At this point I could tell the teacher was past caring about me and attempted to avoid resting her eyes in my direction. Out of desperation, I broke the code of silence to ask about going to the bathroom. I recall the teacher rolling their eyes before telling me no. I attempted to wait, but the matter was becoming more pressing, and I asked again. I was told to be quiet and stop looking for attention. I sat back down and grew silent.

It's remarkable how long time takes to pass when you are desperate. I sat at that desk, stomach cramping, staring at the clock. I truly made every effort to make it to the break. I could not. I sat there, looking down as tears of humiliation streamed down my face as I urinated in my chair.

The teacher discovered the puddle surrounding my desk. She made sure every student in the classroom knew about it as she broke the silence and asked me where it came from. I refused to answer her, so she filled in the blanks for the students by announcing that it appeared I had peed myself in class. I sat in the chair mortified as my hot red cheeks gave away my embarrassment.

It was yet another phone call and parent teacher conference. The teacher told my parents that I had intentionally urinated on myself for attention. At no point was I asked for input, a reason, or excuse. The parental units were told that they needed to manage me better if I was to stay in school. I had detention in the principal's office for a week to prove I was serious about changing my attitude. When we got home, I was humiliated all over again by Mother, who refused to hear my pleas for understanding, making me hand wash my skirt and underwear, telling me how ridiculous I was for not "holding it," and that I deserved what I got.

If I hadn't been deemed an outcast already, I would have been after that. Even the teacher grew colder towards me. I had student after student taunt and tease me. I heard so many comments about being so stupid I couldn't even hold my piss that I grew callous to them. To the outsider, it seemed as though I did not care, or maybe they thought I was too stupid to care. On the inside I felt like a neglected dog, ready to accept anyone who would give the slightest hint of kindness but finding no one.

This continued on through most of my remaining time there. It blossomed into other taunts about having braces, being dirty, being poor, or being fat. The taunt that still resonates all these years later came from when I was in 5th grade. To this day "fatty fatty two by four, couldn't get through the kitchen door" resonates in my head. This was followed by various nasty comments about how I acquired my food while making pig noises at me.

I ended up eating in the bathroom to avoid most of the comments during our breaks, save the ones from the popular girls who found me tucked away in my refuge. They would stride in, flipping their hair, looking me up and down with looks of disgust. They would turn to each other and comment out of their perfect little mouths that I had to eat in the bathroom otherwise I'd piss myself. Continuing in front of me like I didn't exist, talking about how gross I was for eating in a bathroom where people would shit, or numerous other comments that cut deep into my psyche. They would finish what they were doing and saunter out of the bathroom, proud of the knives they left gouged into my soul.

I never told anyone. It didn't matter. The teachers didn't care. The parental units did not care. The students were ruthless, seeing the wounded and going for blood before walking away. They would boast about the emotional torment they bestowed on me. I stood silent, wanting to die, but refusing to succumb to any of them.

Hope Doran

WEIGHT, WHAT?

Ah, weight... something that from a social standpoint should not matter, but oh how it does!! It is the difference between having friends or not, being accepted into social circles, or not, being picked first or last. In my case, it also included being ridiculed by my mother. When all was said and done, I don't think it would have been different if I had been thin. Being heavy was just another thing for her to nit-pick at me over.

Let me tell you, if I wasn't self-conscious enough over my weight, it escalated hard core. Mother had, yet again befriended a woman whose son was in my class. We really did not care for each other. Nevertheless, there we were, forced into each other's company. He thrived on this fact, and would often share tidbits of truth, or fiction about me with our classmates that would leave me scarlet with embarrassment.

When I was forced by Mother's friendship to spend time with the boy, he spared no opportunity to make me feel uncomfortable and unwanted. There were several times he would wander off with one of the neighborhood girls and together they would ditch me. When they weren't doing that, they were showing me Kama Sutra books that she had smuggled out of her mother's bedroom. They would be talking about sex as if they had both experienced it, but as we were 9 and 10 years old, I doubted it. They asked if I liked sex, who I liked in school, and who I wanted to have sex with. I had no answer for them, so they made up stories about me, taking these lies to school. I was really in a no-win situation.

One time, while at his house, the mothers were talking about us. His mother commented on how heavy he was but felt that he would grow into his weight. My mother piped in, saying that was likely, but she was not sure about me seeing as girls develop differently, and she thought I was heavier than the boy. The two women cackled over this before sending us to the scales.

He weighed in first, at just over 100 pounds. Then it was my turn. I didn't want to get on the scale, but Mother insisted. I hesitantly stepped onto the cool metal platform, red with embarrassment. My head dropped down to see my number. I was 109 pounds. I slipped off, keeping my head down as Mother proceeded to exclaim with jubilance that she was right, I was heavier than the boy. As we retraced our steps back into the living room, the mothers commented on how unfortunate it was for me being the fat one.

I was mortified, furious, and filled with hate towards both of them and their thoughtless words and actions towards me. I slipped into their game room, and started pacing around their pool table, rolling the balls around as I walked. I was ashamed not just over my weight, but also over having a mother that would turn me into a joke. I wished I were someone else, somewhere else, with someone else as my mother.

I gathered a pool ball in my hand, feeling its cool

smooth surface turn warm under my palm. I cocked my arm back and threw the ball as hard as I could towards the wall. The ball stuck into the wall briefly before it fell to the ground and slowly rolled back towards the table. I stood frozen in fear, listening for their steps into the game room, but the two women were still too busy laughing at my expense to have heard the impact. Slowly I relaxed, realizing they were oblivious, and walked up to the wall. There, in the perfect paint I stuck my finger into the hole I had made. I removed my hand and looked at the chalky debris that clung to my hand before floating to the floor like snow. I didn't care about what I had done. I found out later the boy got blamed for it. I remember thinking smugly that he deserved it.

We went home and the diet began. Mother was keyed into everything I ate. She was determined to make me thin at any costs. She would mark the milk container so she could monitor how much milk I drank. She would count the slices of cheese. She monitored where she put things in the refrigerator and would verbally attack me about what I had eaten if they were moved. She would comment on the clothes I wore and would talk about how much better they would fit if I lost some weight. She would watch me as I ate. She never missed a moment to comment on the state of my weight.

Thanks to the boy, school was ruthless, and I continued to suffer. My classmates would leave things on my desk to poke fun at me. Things like cupcake wrappers with the crumbs of cake adhered to the pretty paper, bags of vegetables with notes saying things like "here fatty." They all seemed to think it was so funny breaking my spirit one nasty prank at a time, but really it was making me more resilient. I didn't know it at the time but looking back I see it all very clearly.

My embarrassment over my weight took a toll. I started throwing my lunch into the bushes on my way to school. I would hide behind rocks as the school bus drove by, so I didn't have to hear the cutting comments from kids hanging out of the partially opened windows as they went by. Mother was informed that I was not coming to school with lunch. She was furious. She said it made her and Father look like they weren't taking care of me. From then on, she had me check in with the teacher and show my lunch to them.

Well, it got to the point where Mother won. I didn't want to eat. This ended up being something that has threaded its way in and out of my life. I think it was my way of taking back control in a world where I felt I had none. She was hugely satisfied for a period of time because I thinned out. That was replaced with irritation because she could not make me eat. For a while I would eat to shut her up, then go to the bathroom and throw it up. This was my first run with anorexia, but it would not be my last.

MISSING BIKE

Things progressed at school. Other students came in that were considered fresh meat for ridicule, and I slowly faded into the recesses of student's minds. I was fine with this. It was better to be ignored. I welcomed the silence that came with it.

Tetherball was my favorite school pastime, and I became quite good at it. Despite not being particularly liked, I was the one to beat at the game. I dominated during recess and was mostly assured I'd be playing the length of the break.

Schoolwork was another story. I hated school, and most everything that came with it. It's not that I wasn't smart. I was very intelligent. It was more about not being given the graces to develop those scholastic talents. I was a burden to everyone. To the parental units I was someone to deal with, not someone to love. To the teachers, I was someone to scrape through, so they didn't have to see me again or address my "attitude" while under their tutelage. No one seemed to believe in me, so it was hard to believe in myself.

I had headed home for the day. Mother had a system worked out with the teacher, so she knew what homework I had to do. She asked where my English reading book was. I didn't have it. She sent me back to school to retrieve it, telling me I had thirty minutes to get to the school and back. I left the house and headed out on my bike.

Getting down to the school was easy enough as it was all downhill. I got to my classroom and retrieved my book, exiting on the playground side where the tetherball court was. I strode up to the ball, swinging it around by its rope. I took a couple of serves so strong that I stood back and watched the rope bind itself against the pole at its highest point. Sometimes it paid off being tall.

I stepped out of the court and bent down to gather my book for the bike ride home. As my head came up, I saw Steve coming towards me. He was one of the few that was distant but left me alone. I was surprised when he asked to play. My book dropped to the ground as I happily said yes. It was the first time anyone in my class had spoken to me kindly, and I cherished the moment.

We played a few games. I won them all. He walked with me to the front of the school, and we stood awkwardly for a few moments. He looked at me and said, "You're pretty cool, thanks for playing." I stammered a thank you and we parted ways.

I didn't notice the time until I got on my bike. I had been gone for over an hour. Immediate dread filled me as I realized I was in trouble. I biked toward home as quickly as I could, but the panic was building. I rattled my brain with good reasons to have been late. I came up with the best my 9-year-old mind could rummage together. I ditched the bike in one of the many fields I frequented, and ran home.

Running up the long driveway, I focused on the massive fear of retaliation for being late and began crying. I burst through the front door gasping for air, telling Mother three men had stolen my bike. My tears were real, but for the wrong reason. Nevertheless, Mother believed me. I was relieved and escaped into my bedroom.

My feeling of safety was short lived though. Mother immediately called law enforcement. I did not expect that. They told her they would come out to the school tomorrow to interview me. I was nervous. I went to bed pondering telling the truth, but literally terrified of my mother. I fell into fitful sleep, having decided to continue in my lie.

It was yet another day I dreaded going to school. My wait was not long. I was called out from class to the office. I dragged my feet, but they still managed to navigate me to my final destination. I said hello to the officers and sat down.

I regaled them with my tall tale of three men stealing my bike. I could conjure no tears with this tale. I had to make this believable. I had to focus. I had them on board until my story started changing. That's the thing with lies; it's hard to keep the story straight. Try as I might, I couldn't do it. The officers gave each other a knowing look that I now realize is the 'this is total bullshit' look. When I was done, they sent me back to class.

I finished out my day, and my walk home was uneventful. I was uneasy, but I heard nothing back from anyone, so by the end of the school day I had relaxed a bit. I meandered home making note of nature's subtle changes which had occurred since my walk to school. I slowed as I came across the area where I had dumped my bike. I should have seen it from the road, but it was not visible. My heart sank as I lost my last bit of hope of retrieving the bike and taking it home to claim I had found it by the side of the road. I wondered what had happened to it.

I tentatively entered the house. Father was already home, which was not normal. He and Mother were sitting at the massive dining room table. They asked me to sit down with them. My hands became immediately clammy as I sank into the chair. Mother asked if there was anything I wanted to tell them. 'Hell no' was all my inside voice yelled, but outwardly I whispered "no." Mother said fine. She and Father stood, walked to the door and ushered me into the van.

We began a trek that appeared to head into the small town we frequented on the weekends. Mother said we were headed to the sheriff's office. I did not know what to think. I thought perhaps they had found my bike and would be returning it to me and that would be the end of things. I was halfway right, they had found the bike all right, but that was not the end of things.

Soon we were seated in the deputy's office. It was a very small space, and we piled in. I sat in the chair across from the officer while the parental units stood behind me. I could hear Mother's breathing. It was short and checked as she maintained her composure, but I knew what that really meant. I was in trouble.

The officer told me they had found my bike after interviewing people in the several homes between the school and our house. My stomach dropped. He then told me that an individual had watched me deposit my bike on his property before leaving for home. The individual said nothing of three men. I of course knew this. My fear building, I recanted my story, telling them I was trying to stay out of trouble because I had been gone too long to retrieve my book. I told them I was scared of my mother and what she would have done. I tried my best to plead my case, but in the end, I was not heard.

In hindsight, I now understand that what a 9-year-old says in explaining abuse often does not translate appropriately to an adult ear. The sheriff was no exception. He mentally placed me into the rebellious group and scolded my parents. He told them, "If you can't control her at 9, how the hell do you expect to control her at 15?" I desperately wanted assistance. I wanted to tell him of my woes, breaking each moment down until he saw things from my perspective. Even at 9, I knew this was impossible.

I sat in silence. I heard that I had taken several officers off a major murder case. I had recalled hearing something about that in the news and felt bad for causing trouble. The officer continued, stating he felt he should place me in juvenile detention. He said against his better judgment, he would not. Instead, he said I would have a record that would be sealed, and if I turned 18 without any further instances of illegal activity, my record would be expunged.

As we left his office, Father had me reach for the door. When I opened it, he made note of that, telling me next time I might not be so lucky, and the door may be locked. That night my discipline changed. The belt was no longer effective for them, so I was hit with a cutting board. It was the complete scenario, bend over, grab my ankles, and offer my ass up for a mother of all whoopings. I couldn't sit comfortably for days. I don't recall how many times I was hit, but every time I released my grasp from my ankles, the count started over. I was massively bruised on the back of my thighs and ass. That cutting board haunted me well into adulthood, but that's a story for later.

HAPPY BIRTHDAY!

I was turning ten!!! Even with no friends to really call my own, I was excited to be in the double digits! Two whole hands! I reveled in this, and my heart pounded with excitement. I wondered what I was getting for my birthday. Mother had said I would really like it. I was practically giddy.

When it came to birthdays, Mother had a ridiculous tradition. She would not pile up the gifts as one normally does, allowing the receiver to take in their newly acquired gift set. She would keep them concealed in her room, bringing them out, one at a time. In addition to that, each gift had a time on it. That was when I would be allowed to open the gift. She said that was a way of prolonging the excitement of the day. It had the opposite effect on me. I grew irritated at the gift I was required to hold and walk around with for sometimes up to two hours.

More times than not, birthdays were used as a day to gift me with socks or underwear, under the pretense of being something I wanted. To my young mind, her fake excitement over necessities fell off me like a dead fly from a fly swatter. That was compounded by the fact I didn't know how many gifts there were, or how close I was to being done. It really was not fun as I opened gift after gift wishing it were something amazing like Troll dolls that were so popular, or Hot Wheel cars that I had grown so fond of. Decorative wrapping would fall to the floor only to find a pair of cotton underwear or socks I definitely did not want for a birthday gift.

Regardless of this, I held hope for my tenth birthday. Mother rarely toted her gifts, so it ignited excitement in me. She started with her normal banter over prolonging the birthday event and began bringing out the gifts. I had learned from previous experience not to let my frustration show. I sat and waited for the open time for each gift. 10:17, socks, 12: 29, underwear. She brought out the third gift for me in a tiny box with her perfect scripted writing that said 1:42. I waited. At the appropriate time I opened the box.

Inside the box was another even smaller box that said open at 3:00. I got nothing for the 1:42 gift time. She smirked at me, and I could hide it no more. I sullenly went to my room. She told me to take the box with me. I picked it up and chucked it at the wall when I entered the safety of my closed bedroom door.

Mother called me out at 3:00. I flung myself off my bed, grabbed the box off the floor and sauntered into the living room. She excitedly told me to open the box. I lowered my head so she could not see the deep roll of my eyes as I proceeded to disclose the contents of the box. It was again, Mother's refined penmanship, this time revealing the gift of painting my bedroom any color of my choosing. At last, I was excited!!

I quickly landed on purple as I held the next gift in my hand. This one was to open at 4:45. Mother was vehemently opposed to the color purple, and my excitement quickly waned. I didn't understand why I couldn't have what I wanted. Shit, she was the one who said I could have what I wanted! By the time 4:45 came around, I was crushed, and my room was to be painted a light shade of green.

I opened my last gift defeated. Inside was a note that said to go outside to the old oak tree. I obliged, without enthusiasm. Out back my father was standing beside the massive Oak, holding something back above him. I came up to the Oak and he smiled, letting go of a tire swing. I watched as it swayed back and forth. I was told that was my last gift, and the parental units went inside and left me out with the swing.

I dove into the center of the tire, flipping my body around to settle my bottom into the swing. I sat in the tire for a while, its rubbery scent embalming me in its embrace. I kicked my feet into the dirt and leaves, slowly propelling myself forward. As my body started swaying back and forth, I would kick the ground as I came back to center. When I got ample air, I let the tree take me where it would, tears of frustration and disappointment cooling my hot cheeks.

Years later I would write a poem about my Oak. That swing ended up being one of my favorite gifts in my entire childhood. That tree held treasures for me in the form of comfort, solitude, and peace. It goes to show that just because you don't get what you want, it doesn't mean you won't have something you cherish. I cherished that Oak. She was my lifeline. It was a good lesson learned.

MY OAK

The air is crisp as I exhale its frosty sharpness.

I see my breath muting the swing as I stride to it.

My bare feet accepting the dead, prickly oak leaves

As I close the distance... crunch, crunch.

I slide into the tire swing, and My Oak accepts me with a slight groan.

She knows my secrets and steals them away within her memories.

Holding them fast as I spin and spin.

My tears scatter beneath My Oak as I circle around.

I water My Oak, giving her life as she saves mine... crying, crying.

I breathe deep, taking in the winter air

Gasping as I expand into a full swing.

Reaching for a new sky, new air, new life.

My Oak swings with me,

Guiding me to something new, fresh, caring.

Gently guiding me to peace, tranquility, acceptance.

My Oak slowly adjusts as my swinging stops.

Her leaves shelter me, some falling on me like a gentle caress.

As I walk back to the house, I hear My Oak whisper... there, there.

And I know I will be alright.

TO GRANDMA'S HOUSE I GO

We hadn't seen Grandma hardly at all since my family portrait was done. Rest assured; my grandma was still just as important to me. As summer before I turned 11 came into full swing, the parental units were looking for something to occupy my time. I could hear them discussing things but couldn't ever quite hear what they were saying. I did my best to stay out of their way.

It turned out that Grandma wanted me to spend a couple of weeks with her before school started. Mother agreed to let me go, but Mother imposed some very strict rules. She sat me down and very sternly said we needed to talk. She proceeded to tell me they were allowing me to go to grandmother's house. She said that I was in no way, shape, or form to accept any gifts from Grandma. She said I was not to ask for anything, and if she found out that I had, I would be disciplined. She told me this was a test, and I needed to pass it if I was to spend any more time with Grandma after this. I eagerly agreed to her terms, and we were off to grandma's house the following day.

The ride to Grandma's always seemed to take forever in my young mind. I sat as patiently as possible, not wanting to rile Mother up and have her change her mind. Before too long, we arrived. The parental units had something to eat before heading back, leaving me in my favorite space with my favorite person.

Things started out slow enough. We hung out at grandma's house or at the nearby swimming pool. I loved it. Grandma would play cards with me, make me sandwiches or my favorite pastime, playing dress up in all her clothes and then crawdad fish from her backyard. While in her care, I felt a huge wave of relief wash over me, and I began to relax. For a small window of time, everything was wonderful.

Before too long, Grandma started asking me what else I wanted to do. With Mother's words sharp in my memory banks, I quickly told her nothing. I said I was happy to just be there with her. She persisted, saying there must be things I wanted to do, and I slowly started to open up, asking to go roller skating, or go out to eat, to buy art supplies so I could draw her pretty things. In my mind the last one at least offered something to her, so I would probably be okay with that. We had so much fun doing all of these; I almost forgot Mother's rules until Grandma offered to take me shopping for back-to-school clothes. I panicked.

I regaled Grandma with the rules Mother had laid out. I told her I was already going to be in so much trouble because Grandma had done so much for me already. I was becoming hysterical with fear. Grandma saw that. She reassured me, telling me not to worry. She said she wouldn't tell Mother about our outings. She said she wanted to take me shopping, and not to worry, that she would take care of Mother.

Feeling safe with Grandma's promise, I said okay. We headed out for yet another day of fun. Grandma spoiled me with so many clothes, shoes, and school supplies. I was ecstatic. My favorite gift was a Mickey Mouse watch with a blue wristband. I was excited to be going back to school dressed fashionably. It was going to be the first time that had ever happened.

The parental units picked me up a few days later. The fear that had been sitting in the back of my mind exploded within me, and my hands were trembling from my racing heart. I was panicking. I had tried to pack everything into the bag I had come with. Shoving my precious new things into every bit of space I could find. Try as I might, Grandma's generosity was too extensive, and there was no way everything was going to fit. I entered the living room with two bags. Mother quickly caught sight of them and asked what they were. I remained silent and looked to Grandma as Mother watched from behind narrowed eyes.

Grandma proceeded to tell Mother I had filled her in regarding the agreement, but she just wanted to have some time with me and spoil her grandchild. She said it was not my fault; I had done as Mother instructed. Grandma told Mother if she wanted to be mad, be mad at her and not me. Grandma's plea fell on deaf ears as Mother loaded up my things and told me to get into the vehicle.

She and Grandma exchanged words in front of the vehicle, but I could not understand what was said. I did see the look on Grandma's face, and I knew it wasn't good. Mother got into the vehicle, and we drove off. She informed me that seeing as I could not keep my boundaries with Grandma, I wouldn't be spending time with her anymore.

She said she hoped I had a good time, because it was the last time I'd be alone with her.

We got back to the house and Mother demanded to see what I had acquired. I showed her the school supplies, clothes, shoes, and the watch. She scoffed, saying it was a waste of money. Mother told me she hoped I liked what I got, because she would not be buying me any clothes for a long time. I accepted my punishment, silently thanking Grandma for a brief moment where I could at least feel like I fit in. They were the nicest clothes I had ever had.

Mother meant what she said though. I only saw Grandma one other time before I turned 18. It was at Christmas. I had missed Grandma so much, and I know she missed me too, but it wasn't the same. Mother had gotten to her. Our relationship was enveloped in Mother's manipulation. The outcome was so intense, even Grandma couldn't escape it.

CLEAN YOUR ROOM

I loved the things Grandma got me. It was nice to be happy in what I was wearing. At every turn Mother made one comment or another about not liking them. It all fell on deaf ears. When that didn't work, she took to other methods.

I was never great at keeping things clean in my room. It was never horrible, but there were always scatterings of things on the floor and the closet was unkempt. I had been taught how to do laundry at nine years old, and from that point on, I was in charge of doing my own. I didn't mind doing the laundry but hated folding clothes. As a result, oftentimes the clothes were left scattered around on the floor.

Mother hollered at me to clean my room. I said okay but was lost in thought. Next to being outside, my room was usually a space to daydream more than to be productive. Most times the parental units left me alone, not wanting to stir me out of my space. I busied myself with playing in my room, and half ass cleaning up. The end result was stacking my clothes, unfolded on the closet shelf.

I readied myself to go into town with Father to run errands. I came out of my room and headed to the already running van outside. Father was eager to go. As my hand reached for the doorknob to go outside, Mother asked if my room was clean. With the question was the threat that she would be sure it was clean while I was gone. I muttered a yes and left out the door, scampered into the van, and we headed to town.

I always enjoyed going into town. It didn't really matter what we were in town for. It was a breath of fresh air, and a time to relax during the 30-minute ride to the outskirts of our little town of Santa Cruz. Time spent in town was always too short. We did our errands, and soon were headed back to the house. When we returned home, I helped Father unload the groceries. We brought everything in and put it all away. I always enjoyed grocery days. It let me know what we had to eat for the week. Mother was nowhere to be seen. I went to my room.

Initially, I didn't notice much. The room seemed tidier than when I left, but that went over my head. I went to get one of my toys, and noticed it was not there. That's when I started to look around and noticed lots of things were gone. I went into the closet to be sure I didn't put things in there, and noticed a lot of my clothes were gone. I freaked out, looking in every crack and crevice for them. I went out to the back deck where the washer and dryer lived. Both were empty.

Mother came sauntering out from her bedroom, watching me as I came back from the back porch. I asked her if she knew where my things were. She said yes. I asked her where they were, and she told me they were in the trash. When I spun around to go retrieve them, she yelled at me. She said the loss was my fault because I had been warned that she would throw away anything that wasn't put away. I pleaded with her, telling her they were put away. She stared at me, telling me they weren't put away properly (enunciating properly for effect). She told me if I pulled them out of the trash, I would get the board. And with that, I lost most of the clothes Grandma had gotten me.

Hope Doran

CHURCH

I walked past the tiny church all the time. I didn't really know much about church or religion. I happened past it one Sunday while escaping the house and headed to parts unknown. I sat in the recesses of the property, watching people collect inside the tiny building. I would listen to the singing, and it filled me with peace. That was a new feeling for me. I liked it. I began finding myself sitting outside the church weekly. I would sit against a tree, listening to greeters welcoming everyone in. There would be prayers, hymns, and the welcoming of each other back to the church.

My favorite part came after the singing. The kids were dismissed and ushered to another room for Sunday School. This was not like the schooling I was accustomed to. This school looked and sounded like fun! There were projects, more singing, and discussion over things in the Bible. I didn't understand any of this, but I wanted to be a part of it. I started going to church by myself. It was the first time I recalled being socially bold.

I was proud of my decision. I loved the feeling of freedom while I was there. Oddly, no one seemed to question a young child coming to the church alone. Everyone always had a smile for me and welcomed me in. I loved the singing, and quickly learned the hymns, singing them loudly, letting the music flood and heal my broken heart.

It was a place where I felt like I fit in and belonged. I felt better when I went. It was a small escape I had from my house during the weekends. There were even other kids that I went to school with that were nice to me there. Slowly, that branched out to school as well. I was beginning to feel a little better. I didn't know it at the time, but I was beginning to heal.

This went on for months undetected. I enjoyed the freedom my church offered. I think the parental units were just as happy to have me out of the house as I was to be out of it. It was a good arrangement I had made for myself, until winter came around. Mother questioned why I was going out when it was raining and cold. I had to decide whether or not to disclose something that had become precious to me. I knew if I didn't, she would say no, and tell me to stay at the house, so I gave up my prized location.

Mother sat, awestruck. I could tell she wanted to be upset, but over what? It was church. I had learned enough of church by now to know it was a good thing and my only possible indiscretion was that I didn't tell her sooner and let her assume I was wondering about the forest. My secrecy was a way to maintain something that I had grown to love and enjoy. Those tended to be things Mother liked to strip away from me.

Mother lurched out of her chair. She stood, pale and swaying, letting the blood seep to the parts of the body allowing for further movement. She looked at Father, then at me and stated with hostility that we were all going to church. Shocked, I pondered why Mother would want to attend church. They were never interested, and they hadn't even married in a church. I sat and waited impatiently in my jeans, t-shirt, and jacket as they readied themselves in their current finest.

As we exited the vehicle, I was embarrassed. Not for my flat attire compared to the parental units, but because of their presence. They followed me around the church as though they were my shadow, stitched to my very being. I said hello to friendly faces and introduced the parental units to them in a veiled attempt of normalcy. Mother's thin lips were pursed in displeasure when she wasn't forcing a smile towards my fellow church members. Even I could see the disapproval through the plastered smile. My soul crumbled. I knew right then and there she was going to take my church away from me.

We started with hymns. I sang my heart out like it was the last time I'd be in this beautiful space. Tears coming down my face as I belted out "It Is Well" as loud as my little voice would go. Then there was the pastor, welcoming in everyone, taking note of those who were new, stating what a pleasure it was to finally meet the parental units. With that, he excused us kids.

I leaped out of my seat in relief. Finally, my escape! That was short lived as Mother got up with me. I told her I was going to Sunday school. She said, "Yes, and I'm going with you." I fought back the tears as she followed me out of the church and into the small classroom. We all sat, Mother in the corner, scrutinizing every little thing. I participated as much as possible, trying to show Mother this was a good thing, something I could learn from, take pride in, something that would make me a better person. My attempts were in vain.

At the end of church, the parental units openly discussed the church activities. They did not approve. They went so far as to say what the church taught was demonic, and not of the Lord. For the life of me, what she said made no sense. What did they know about church anyway? In all my young years I had never seen either of them go to church, or even pick up a Bible. I watched as the two of them verbally destroyed my sanctuary. When we got home, I went to my room and cried.

That was the end of my little church. They never let me go back. It did ignite the Righteous Wrath of Jesus Christ in them though. The two of them decided on a new church to attend. They both became zealous for the Lord, and I definitely paid the price. My religious sanctuary became a world where to spare the rod is to spoil the child, which is framed in the *Bible*, book of Proverbs 13:24. The parental units thoroughly embraced this and welcomed the opportunity to take the verse quite literally. They finally had the excuse they needed to beat the shit out of me as a form of discipline and have, in their opinion, the full support of their new Lord in doing so.

MISSIONETTES

The new church did come with some perks. I was allowed to go to Sunday School, which did not feel as safe, but I welcomed the absence of Mother. I observed as the parental units immersed themselves into the Pentecostal Christian faith. They became saved, full believers in the Lord Jesus Christ, speaking in tongues, and dancing in the Spirit within the church aisles. They were officially Holy Rollers.

I embraced my new position. It was nice to be accepted. I was still odd to others. I was still a tomboy that the pastor misgendered when we met, but things were mostly okay. The church was quite a drive to get to, but the parental units were more than eager, both in their newfound righteousness and the hope that I would finally turn out the way they thought I should.

There were youth programs available at the church. Missionettes being one specifically for young girls. It could be compared to Girl Scouts in that there were badges to earn, things to read, and presentations to give. Everything within the program centered on Christianity. I was slow to start, but enjoyed the company of other girls my age that were, for the most part nice. It wasn't long before I welcomed the biweekly outings to the church.

The Missionettes program was designed to last for between 3 and 5 years. Badges were earned toward the completion of the program in addition to the other badges that could be earned for things such as etiquette, cooking, helping others, along with many, many others. I earned several badges in addition to the program badges. It was challenging in that the program seemed designed to foster competition under the pretense of supporting one another. There were definite overachievers that reveled in showing everyone up. It created a divide among us girls, and there were some bitter moments as a result. By the end of the program, I could not wait to be done.

Missionettes had a summer church camp yearly that celebrated the girls who had completed the program. They were named Honor Stars. The camp was filled with between 200 to 300 girls, with only a small handful being crowned as Honor Stars. The year I was crowned there were about 15 girls receiving the same honor. It was an accomplishment to complete the program, and we were very excited.

The event required a beautiful white dress, similar to a wedding dress. Hell, they were wedding dresses. Surprisingly, Mother took me out to find a dress, but as usual, it was on her terms. Other dresses I had seen in the past were smooth satin that shimmered in the fluorescents of the church lights. Mother would have no such thing. I ended up with a dull, itchy, laced dress that fit my mood. I didn't understand why I couldn't have what I wanted, but Mother said satin was for lingerie, and inappropriate for a church celebration.

My attitude over my appearance in the upcoming event was further dampened by my new haircut. I had not done well with my school grades and on occasion Mother had taken to cutting my hair as discipline. It seemed as though she enjoyed seeing my spirit crushed. That was something that no longer happened when I was hit with the cutting board because I would focus on my pent-up anger, rage, and feelings of entrapment. I would bend over, grab my ankles, and take the slicing of the cutting board without emotion. It served me well, but the lack of reaction was met with simmering anger within the parental units. Instead, she had sent me into town with Father for my disciplinary haircut. I was mad, and hated the cut, but was grateful it was still a little bit long, and breathed a sigh of relief as we headed home.

Upon walking in the door to the house, Mother charged up to me and inspected my hair. She scowled in disappointment and said, "That looks like a 'C' grade haircut, wouldn't you agree?" I watched her dumbfounded as Mother retreated to her bathroom. I stood at the front door frozen for what was coming next. She briskly returned which shears, grabbed my arm, ushered me into the kitchen and sat me down in a chair. She proceeded to hack at my hair for several minutes before retreating a step back to admire her handiwork. Pleased, she spun on her heels and left me alone in the kitchen.

I hesitantly stood, afraid to look in the mirror. I was bathed in locks of hair that encircled my feet and dangled from my shoulders and clothes. I knew it was short, very short. I slowly walked to my room and closed the door. The mirror above the dresser spared no expense as it reflected my ugly truth. It was horrendous. My remaining hair was awful, short, uneven, and ugly. I looked at my reflection like

I was looking at a broken soul. I pitied that girl. I was angry with her for not fighting back even though I knew she had no power to fight… Not right then anyway.

So that's how I went to the ceremony. I attended in a dress I hated with hair I hated and a life I hated. It was written all over my face. I was supposed to be in the center of all the Honor Stars for the yearly photo, but the photographer switched me with my friend Shannon, who had long hair, smiling beautifully in her shimmering satin dress. A sea of happy girls surrounded me. Girls that looked up to me for what I accomplished, but the joy over my accomplishment was lost. I was at that age where I started to care even more about my appearance, and Mother knew it. She cut me emotionally and permanently scared me. I believe she was proud of that moment. It sure seemed that way. To this day I hate how I look with short hair. It still makes me cry.

MY CLOTHES

I hated the clothes Mother got me for school. I was lucky if they were new. Forget about fashionable. Long gone were the clothes Grandma gifted me with. I was so tired of acting as though I was appreciative when really, I just wanted to hide. She loved to take me to consignment stores. Let me first say it wasn't the fact that the clothes were used, it was the fact that her new favorite consignment store had a clientele that likely had a median age of 60.

Mother happily took me to the store. I quickly realized I was being dressed in some random grandma clothes because she really liked the clothes there. It was an opportunity for her to slip in things for herself when she was claiming to be shopping for me. It was dreadful. She would occasionally look at me sideways and say something like, 'that looks really nice on you." It always seemed to be the things I detested the most, and often was what I went home with as mine.

There were two events that sent me over the edge as far as my clothing goes. One was my aunt's wedding. I was excited to go. I had my outfit picked out, which included new high heels I had acquired for my Missionettes ceremony. I sauntered out to the living room feeling pretty in my clothes, tinted lip gloss, and high heeled shoes. I remember feeling a little grown up. Mother took one look at me and said one word, "no." I pleaded with her to let me wear it, but she insisted, telling me to wear one of the dresses she had purchased from the consignment store.

I was crushed. I went back to my room and began disrobing. I sat in my pantyhose and bra on the bed sulking. The parental units grew impatient to leave and Mother came and chose a gray polyester dress for me to wear. She tossed it on the bed and told me to get ready, or I wouldn't be going. I put it on, and we left.

The wedding was beautiful. One bright moment to it was the realization that I had donned the same color as the wedding party, so I felt like I fit in. Unfortunately, the pictures do not depict any enjoyment from me. Once, while looking through the wedding photos with my aunt, I came across one with me in it. I could see the attitude all over my face. I could only imagine how that came across on my aunt's special day. My attitude had ruined at least one photo, likely more.

The other occasion was my graduation from middle school. It was around the same time as the Honor Star ceremony, and I wanted to wear the dress to graduation. Not because I loved the dress, but because I had heard other people talking about what they would be wearing. Girls were describing these huge fancy formal dresses they would be donning, and I once again thought it would be nice to fit in.

I literally begged Mother to allow me to wear the dress. She scoffed at me. Despite my telling her repeatedly that several other girls were wearing something formal. She still refused; telling me there was no way a parent would dress their child that fancy for an 8th grade graduation. With that she went into my closet and pulled out a dress that she demanded I wear. Stripped of my choice, my eyes fell on my least favorite dress.

It was a rough, itchy polyester dress. Not the kind that is smooth, the kind that you can't wait to get off. It was white, striped with green and blue extending down the length of the dress. Its neckline was a tied off bow to the side, halfway up my neck under my chin. To complete the look was a sash belt of the same material. It was hideous.

I went to the graduation hating my appearance. Once again, it showed in my photos. Even smiling, my eyes are dull, not matching the corners of my mouth. The graduation procession was laden with boys in three-piece suites. Girls were attired in stunning full ball gowns and others dressed in simple, pretty dresses. I looked like I was in a fashion show for the elderly. When the ceremony was complete, Mother strode up to me. Taking inventory of the crowd, she said, 'huh, it looks like the girls were dressed up after all." I would have punched her if I could have gotten away with it.

That summer I held down odd and end jobs for the neighbors. I gardened at one place and watered the wine grapes for our landlord. It wasn't a lot of money, but I had enough to buy my own clothes by the end of summer. I asked Mother if I could go shopping for clothes on my own. She agreed but said she would not supplement my wardrobe in any way unless it was for birthdays or holidays. I feigned struggling with my decision before agreeing to her terms.

Hope Doran

PLEASE SMOKE

Mother had smoked for years. It was no secret to anyone in the house. She had taken her habit to the great outdoors. She used the excuse of walking the dog. Perhaps thinking out of sight, out of mind. But nothing was lost on either Father or myself. She always smelled of stale smoke, despite being outside. It was just a part of all our lives.

Now that she was rooted in church, Mother began to make changes. One such change was her decision to quit smoking. Steeped in her newfound faith, she began touting that her body was now a temple of the Holy Spirit, and as such, she needed to purify herself. With that, she began her self-purification.

Things seemed pretty par for the course at first. She was euphoric in her decision, so for a time, everything regarding her old ritual was fine. As time went on, her attitude changed. Her words were still ringing out, testifying that she was doing this for the Lord, but everything was going to shit. No one could do anything right. Even Father, who usually melded into her desires, was floundering. He took to being out of the house as much as possible. Oh, how I envied him!

Mother was steadfast in her decision. She had heard of fidget beads to repress nicotine cravings, so she picked some up. For a time, she had them on her person at all times, sliding the green beads around on the satin string.

Those beads became her rosary. Each time she slid a bead across the silky slim rope, it brought her another second of freedom from nicotine, and another step closer to God.

If only that replacement ritual would have worked. She did stop smoking, but she took her rage out on everyone. For once, I was grateful for the homework assigned to me, and I made myself scarce. Her fury was frightening. Unfortunately, I couldn't always escape it.

The parental units had invited their new pastor and his wife over for an early dinner. They sat around the table, gabbing over this and that as we ate. I was itching to get away but knew better than asking to be excused. I waited patiently for everyone to wind down. Finally, Mother excused me to clear the table and do the dishes.

I hated doing the dishes, but it had been my chore since I was 9 years old. I got up, cleared the table of Mother's nicer dishware, and took everything into the kitchen. Once there, I did as I'd been instructed, cleaning everything, making sassy mocking faces into the water's reflection as I mimicked them laughing and talking in the other room. It helped the process go faster, and before I knew it, I was done washing and left them to dry.

The group went for a walk to the end of the driveway, talking about those boring adult things like church, faith, work, families and how things were going. I watched as they retreated from sight around the slight bend in the driveway. I could still hear the faint sound of their voices carry back through the windows of the house.

They were down there for some time, and I went back into the kitchen to finish drying the dishes and put them away. As I came to the end of the dishes, I noticed I was missing a coffee cup. I panicked. I looked everywhere but could not find it. I finally went to Mother.

I walked up to her, waiting for a break in their conversation. She ignored me until it was becoming uncomfortable, finally turning to me asking, "Yes?" I told her I couldn't find one of the cups from her dish set. I could feel the silence settle in the room. The pastor uneasily crossed and uncrossed his legs, and his wife looked around anxiously as Mother's facial expression hardened toward me.

She asked me why I was lying to her, in front of company no less. I told her I wasn't lying; it was missing. She then accused me of breaking the cup and hiding it in the trash. I vehemently denied doing such a thing. She yelled at me, right there, calling me a liar. With that, she flew out of the chair, charged into the kitchen, and started going through all the cabinets, slamming the doors as she went. This was followed by going out to the trash and dumping it out on the ground, yelling at me to go through it and show her everything while looking for the nonexistent broken pieces of a cup.

Once I put everything back in the trash can, I thought I was off the hook. She proceeded to yell at me, asking me where I put the cup. I could see the pastor and his wife scurrying around in the living room collecting their things to leave. I pleaded with her, telling her I didn't do anything with the cup. With the loudest of voices, she screeched at me, telling me to stop lying. She sent me to my room while she attempted to repair the damage she had done with her guests, but it was too late. Before too long they had left.

Mother came back into my room. I could feel the heat of her rage as she asked again where the cup was. I didn't know, and that's what I told her. She left and was replaced by Father, who hit me with the cutting board and sent me to bed. It was hours before I was able to fall asleep. I was so angry with them my body was shaking.

The next day I tried to make myself scarce. Still being convinced I was lying about a cup only served to fuel Mother's anti nicotine rage. I did my homework and slipped outside. I figured I'd be okay if I stayed on the property.

I meandered down to the end of the driveway, sitting up on its banks. As I slid down to walk back, something caught my eye. There, on the other side of the driveway, was the cup. I walked up to it staring at my reflection down in the leftover remains of Father's coffee. I slowly picked up the cup and watched as I tipped over its contents, leaving a muddy brown puddle on the ground.

I took the cup back to the house, thinking I would show Mother, and everything would be made right. I should have just left it alone. She amped back up, now accusing me of hiding the cup so I didn't have to wash it. I asked her why I would lie about one single cup when I cleared and cleaned all the other dishes? Boy was that a mistake. She called Father out to tell him what she thought I had done. He stayed silent, even after I saw the realization of his mistake cross his face. I got grounded for "continuing in my lies" in addition to having been beat the night before. Father never told Mother it was his fault and never apologized to me. I went to my room screaming into my pillow, sobbing as I begged God to please give her permission to smoke.

Hope Doran

DRAMA

Do you ever have moments when you think your life is just completely and utterly boring? I always thought my life was completely drab compared to the lavish stories I would read about. Between the books and seeing what seemed like such wonderful reflections of lives in my fellow students, I felt even more isolated. I had gotten to the point where I truly believed the only life worth talking about was someone, anyone else's.

I was about to embark into the world of junior high. It was a whole new adventure, and I was looking forward to meeting new people, and I really liked the idea of going from one class to the other. It oddly made me feel a little grown up. So, when orientation day came, I was very excited.

The auditorium was packed with incoming 7th graders. The principal went through the standard "welcome to the school" speech, which was followed by the school's student body having a mini rally welcoming us while explaining the process for registering for classes. Before long, they cut us loose to sign up for classes and the times we wanted them. I enjoyed that everything I chose were my decisions. It really lent itself to a feeling of independence.

When all was said and done, I had all my classes. Among them were electives. I was particularly excited for my selection of drama class. I saw it as an opportunity to explore my creative side and embark on being more socially bold. I had pondered my decision before finalizing it, knowing it would involve me coming out of the shell I had encapsulated myself in as protection.

I decided I was ready to imagine life from a different perspective than that of reading or observing other people's seemingly perfect lives. I also thought drama would ease the ache that I held for my own existence. I thought it would be wonderful to envelope myself in a character and act out their life as if it were my own, even if it was only for a moment.

When I got back home, nothing much was said to Mother about the orientation. I mentioned to her that the school seemed fun. I said classes got selected, and talked about how large the school was compared to the elementary school I had just graduated from. I said I was nervous about starting, to which she answered that I was having a normal reaction to change.

On the first day of school, everything seemed a bit hectic. I was grateful I had gone to all the classrooms that would be mine during the orientation. In spite of that, I got caught up in the nervous hustle from the other students frantically slamming fists on locker doors that refused to open, yelling over the heads in the hallway and melding into me as we all wove in and out of each other in an attempt to reach our destinations. Another new experience for me were the few couples that had either quickly paired off, or were already dating, flaunting their relationships with sloppy kisses in the hallway before retreating into their classrooms. I felt like a stranger in a foreign land.

Finally, I made it to the class I was most anticipating, drama. The instructor had us all splay out on the stage as she rattled off the rules of the classroom. She continued, talking about the different productions that would take place during the semester. With that, she discussed tryouts, stating that the acting roles would require more after school time, so we needed to have our parents sign a permission slip to participate in drama class. With that, she handed out the slips just as the bell rang signaling the end of the day.

I loaded up my backpack and headed out. I had a few minutes before the bus left to take all of us "Dooners" back up to our homes in Bonny Doon. I was caught up in the excitement of being back to school, allowing the energy of the others around me to ignite my own excitement in my scholastic and friendship adventures. I finally made my way to the bus, and a short time later we were heading home.

Once I arrived home, Mother asked how my first day of school was. I lightheartedly regaled her with my day. I told her of the classes, and teachers I liked. I saved the best for last, finishing up with telling her about my favorite class, drama. As I was excitedly talking about tryouts for the fall production, I saw Mother's face shift. I disregarded the blatant scowl as I explained my need to have her sign the permission slip that offered me another escape into a world bigger then my own.

I handed her the slip, along with a pen. She looked at it, then at me refusing to take it. Thinking she misunderstood, I told her again that she had to sign it as I shook the pen and paper in front of her. In a lightning moment, she swiped them both from my hand. I stood in awkward, confused silence as I watched her crumble up the permission slip.

She coldly said, "You cannot participate in drama." I stood there, not really knowing how to respond. I was confused as to why she would say no. I stared at her, waiting for more. When it didn't come, I asked her why. She stared me down for a moment, angered that I would challenge her with a question. When she did finally answer, her face was devoid of emotion, but her words cut. She said, "You already know how to lie too well. I'm not going to give you permission to take a class that will teach you how to lie even better than you already do."

I tried to whisper a response, telling her that acting was not lying but she cut me off, telling me to change the elective, or she would change it for me. The following day I withdrew from my drama class and signed up for cooking. I hated it, but I guess it was domestic enough to fit within Mother's framework for me. She was pleased with the change.

THE BIGGEST LIE

We had changed churches to one closer to home. With Missionettes done, I was expected to sit in church with the adults. Ever since the pastor had been out to our house for dinner, I decided I did not care for him, but the parental units thoroughly enjoyed him, and they had all become friends. I always did what I could to stay out of his way. I didn't trust him.

Another change was that I had entered the wonderful world of junior high school. Having had to drop the drama class, I felt a loss of excitement towards school, and resented Mother for not allowing me to take classes that I wanted to. I had made myself even more distant towards her as the days progressed. Mother had attempted to make amends, but I simply had no interest in granting her the appearance that I was okay.

It was during this time that I discovered fun news. I had come home to the parental units sitting in the living room. They asked me to sit down. My heart pounding, wondering once again what I had done, frantically asking if I was in trouble. For once, the answer was no. I eagerly set aside my pre-teen angst and slid into the gliding rocking chair. The pocket of my pants caught on the worn, thinning upholstery as I shimmied myself into a comfortable position. The chair squeaked under my eager swaying as I bobbed back and forth within its tired arms awaiting the news.

Mother cut to the point. Smiling, she asked if I still wanted a baby brother or sister. At 12 years of age, I figured that would not be in the cards for me, but I did, so I said yes. She regaled me with the information that she was pregnant. I was ecstatic! I would finally have someone to share my love with! Someone who would understand with total purity what living within those house walls really meant. Someone I could share in this life with, a sibling, a friend who got me.

Things progressed, and time passed quickly. The parental units gathered things together in preparation. I could tell they were very excited, but even I couldn't contain my excitement. I did wonder if they were ever excited about my pending arrival. I never asked, but from the stories I had been told, I doubted it.

It was a beautiful spring evening when my brother arrived. I was at school when I got called to the office and told not to catch the bus home. The parental units picked me up in the tan van and we hung out in town while we waited for Mother's contractions to come closer together. Finally, it was time to go to the hospital.

We arrived at the tiny hospital and sat for a moment collecting ourselves. Father exited the van and went around to help Mother. I disembarked behind her. Mother was moving slowly, and Father doted on her as I watched. It was a rare moment. It was beautiful.

Mother was ushered into a delivery room. She was very stoic while she was in labor, but I would not have expected anything else. She had wanted me to witness the birth, and I was excited and nervous to be there. One thing Mother had been very good at was teaching me about sex, including the birthing process. Watching the birth was harrowing. It was the first time I felt sympathy pains as I watched my mother's body contort as she gave life to a small human.

There he was, my baby brother, John… He was perfect. I cried. I saw him before Mother did. I've always enjoyed that fact. It's something that will never change, can never be stripped from me. It bonded me to him. He was the first person I loved instantly. I was so proud to be a big sister!

Before we knew it, we were headed home. I was awestruck. I could not get enough of him. I was busy planning all the wonderful adventures we would have. Getting time with him was rough though. It seemed like there was often a reason I couldn't be with him. I never understood why, and it made me sad. Regardless, I cherished him. I sat and watched him, being careful to not disturb him in his sleep as I daydreamed of days when he was older, and we could play together.

The addition of my brother did not distract Mother for long. Before I knew it, I was back in her crosshairs. I don't recall what I did, but Mother was convinced it warranted being hit by the wooden cutting board. It should have been the same as it always was. Bend over, grab my ankles, if I let go, the count starts over.

For whatever reason, this was different. Mother left for one of her many walks while Father set forth to discipline me. For whatever reason Father opted for the belt over the cutting board and told me to come over and lay myself across his lap. I didn't want to, and my fight or flight response kicked in. I ran.

We circled around the couch, him on one side, and me on the other. Round and round, we went. I could see the frustration in his eyes and for whatever reasons it became funny to me. I laughed and laughed as we circled, cackling as he tried lunging at me from the backside of the couch, tipping it over, unsuccessful in his attempt to capture me. We were both brought to a standstill with the return of Mother, who thought things should be done by now. She yelled at me to go into the kitchen before saying something in a fevered tone to Father that I could not understand.

Father came into the kitchen and grabbed the fucking cutting board. Suddenly I wished I had just been still and taken my punishment. I didn't see rage in Father too often, but this was one of those times when I saw it clear as day. He told me to bend over and grab my ankles. I was terrified and obliged without hesitation. He hit me with such force, I was unable to keep the grasp of my ankles, and I fell headfirst into the floor. My head spun with pain. He told me to do it again, muttering that I didn't keep hold of my ankles. He had no mercy as he hit in the same spot as last time, once again leaving me on the floor. I was told to get back up. With my head spinning I got back up, but I could not keep hold of my ankles, so I kept getting hit. By the time it was over, I had been hit several times and sent to bed. I cried as my blazing hot skin warmed the blankets before I fell into a fitful sleep.

I went to school the next day. There was nothing eventful to it. I had the dreaded PE class that ninety-nine percent of the middle school population couldn't stand. Then there's the one percent, who are "perfect" and trounce around, making the rest of us feel even more insecure. The whole idea of stripping down in front of other people was mortifying to me. I would always slink around, trying to change undetected behind a silly excuse of a locker door for privacy.

I worked on switching out my clothes as quickly as I could. I had been beaten so many times in the past I didn't give my appearance much thought until some perky, perfection of a girl walked up to me. She inspected the back of my thighs, saying they were super bruised. She asked what happened to me. Still so desperate to fit in, I mumbled that I didn't know. I didn't want to be the topic of gossip coming out of the lips of people who had no idea what it was really like living in my world. She looked again at my legs, shrugged, and walked away. I stood there in my underwear, holding my sweatpants wondering how bad it looked. I hadn't even looked when I woke up. With the locker room mostly empty, I walked up to the mirror.

I stared at myself for a moment, taking in my reflection with the observance of an outsider. The first thing I noticed was the swelling. I could see it from the front of my legs, which were warped and swollen. The taunt skin of my legs sought to encapsulate my damaged form. As I slowly circled around, I took inventory of the backside of my legs, which had turned into rich, deep shades of purple and blue. The bruises formed perfect angles where the cutting board had made contact. I gasped. It was worse than it usually was. I wanted to kick myself for not digging my nails into my ankles so I wouldn't let go. In the past that had always helped ensure I did not let go as the cutting board made sharp contact with my ass. The ring of the class bell startled me out of my shock, I finished dressing and went to the gym.

I went on with my day, seeping into the mundane, sulking from one class to another. Towards the end of the day, I was called to the office. I did not know why. As I stood up, I could hear the comments coming from the lips of my classmates, falling stale and hot in my ears. I was just so tired of not fitting in. As I exited, I let the door slam behind me, ushering the silence I so desperately wanted.

Once in the office, a woman greeted me who I did not know. She introduced herself and said she was a social worker. She led me into one of the smaller offices and closed the door behind her. She directed me to sit and took the chair across from me. She asked simple questions about school, my home life, hobbies, and interests. I was confused but answered hollowly. Finally, she cut to the point.

"I received a call that you have some pretty bad bruises," she said. I stared at her in disbelief. She asked if I wanted to talk about it. My cheeks flushed and my eyes started to burn with hot tears and my gaze darted to the old red carpeting on the floor. I focused on a brown stain embedded in its fibers and told her I did not want to talk about it. She prodded, telling me she had concerns I was not being treated well, and she had concern for my safety. My tears flowed down my face and into my lap.

I broke down and told her everything. I told her my parents had disciplined me, and that my Father had used a cutting board to hit me. I told her it happened frequently, whenever I did something they did not like. I explained Mother would have Father punish me. I laid it all out on the line. It was my time to be heard. I finally saw a chance to save my brother and me.

She was very receptive to what I was saying, taking notes, asking more questions. I eagerly answered all of them. She wrapped things up with me and left to call in my parents who had been summoned earlier. I waited anxiously for her return, terrified of Mother and her retaliation if she would be able to get to me.

Mother and Father strode into the office. Calm cool and collected. They vehemently denied hitting me with the cutting board. They told her I was lying to her to get attention because they had a new baby and couldn't give me the attention they used to. They told the social worker I was a difficult child, and always had been. The social worker pondered this and told my parents we would need to meet again with someone else to evaluate the situation. My parents agreed to that, but said they wanted to meet at the church we attended so their pastor could be there as well. The social worker said that was fine and excused me to leave with my parental units. She must have seen the fear in my eyes. She hesitated, resting her hand on my shoulder telling me she would be in touch with me tomorrow. We left.

They were contained fury. The drive home was silent, even my infant brother was silent. The silence was deafening. I squirmed around in the backseat, wondering what was next. When we got home, I went to my room and fell into the bed, emotionally exhausted. I did not feel safe. Their silence was enough to tell me they were enraged. Nothing was spoken and I fell into a fitful sleep.

We met the next day after school. The parental units picked me up and we drove the short distance to the new church we were attending. On the way there, Mother said I should really consider what I said. I stared at her wondering what the hell she expected me to say. For the slightest moment I saw the fear in her eyes. It was brief, and then the icy gaze was back. We entered the church.

The pastor was there with two social workers, the woman I'd spoken with at school the day before, and one of her colleagues. They wanted to talk to me alone, and under the pastor's protest, he was not allowed to join us. The pastor then requested a prayer and proceeded to pray that the Lord guide all of us to the proper outcome and that the Lord would guide my heart back into his loving folds of honesty. It was all completely passive aggressive and meant to undermine what I was saying. I stood to exit and go into another room while the parental units and the pastor stared me down, searing my back with their eyes as I made my escape.

The social workers sat me down. It was a repeat of the previous day, making small talk before showing them my bruises and delving into how I got them. I told them everything. When I was finished, they told me to wait in the room as they left to confer with the parental units and the pastor.

The conversation with them was brief, and they came back in, and we all sat at a table. One of the social workers began grilling the pastor about the parental units, asking were they people of integrity? How were they as members of his congregation? The pastor was glowing in his review of them. He stated I was a troubled child, who often required discipline, but he had every confidence the parental units would do that within the confines of a loving nature. I literally scoffed. Mother shot me a dagger of a stare. I coldly stared back at her. She upped the ante.

"My daughter has a history of compulsive lying," she blurted. She continued with regaling them of the time I lied to law enforcement, and how I obviously lacked the ability to discern when a lie was too much, and an unwillingness to admit to my lies and tell the truth. The room grew silent, and all eyes fell on me. I was shocked. "I'm not lying," was all I could say, my face flushed with embarrassment and fear. Hot tears threatened to open their floodgates from my eyes. I looked at the social workers and repeated that I was not lying.

The social workers wanted to talk to me alone again. Mother piped up, saying she wanted to talk to me alone for a moment. She instructed me to follow her outside, and I did. Once outside, she turned to me and told me I didn't know what I was doing. She said I was making a mess out of everything, and I needed to change my story. She told me Father was up for a promotion, and they were doing a background check on him (he now worked for a very large company that was known worldwide). She said he would lose this opportunity, and possibly his job if this became part of his record.

She stared hard into my eyes, searching to see if her words had any impact on me. I didn't care. I wanted to be free of her, of this life she confined me to. Free from years of feeling like she didn't care about me. Free from feeling unloved. Although true, I was furious she had told the social workers about my lying, and my rage showed. She then hit me with the one thing I did care about.

"If you don't change your story, they will take you and your brother away from us. You will not be placed together, and you may never see him again. We may never see either of you again; do you understand what I'm telling you?" She was shaking at this point and had grabbed my shoulders trying to shake her sense into me. I looked at her and she knew she hit her mark. She repeated it again. "You may never see your brother. Is that what you want? Do you want to be separated from him?" My tears now flowed as I sobbed out a no. Knowing she had won, she ushered me back in, pushing me forward back into the room. She sat me down before taking her seat. The room was quiet except for the faint hum of the lights. I sat, tears streaming down my face and tried to collect myself, unsuccessfully.

I changed my story, lying through my teeth. I made up some bullshit about falling or something. I don't even remember what it was I came up with. Initially, the social workers seemed confused, checking their notes. I repeated the lie. I didn't want to lose my brother! I watched the social worker's faces change. It seemed as though they felt they had been duped, but couldn't tell by whom, looking from me to Mother, to each other. I had to keep to the lie. I couldn't lose my brother. The social workers took it all in, dumbfounded, while the pastor sat back in his chair nodding approvingly, as if his prayer had put all this into play. Father looked cautiously at Mother, who sat patiently, waiting for things to play out.

Having the history of lying to law enforcement must have sealed my fate, because soon they packed up everything and we went home. I lost all faith in my ability to set my brother and I free. We were trapped in this web of narcissistic manipulation and lies. The biggest lie I ever told was one of my mother's planning, creating, and executing. She just had to frame it in such a way I would see it as my only option, my only chance to stay with my brother. If I didn't have the history of lying, maybe it would have had a different ending. I lied to protect my brother. I figured I could keep him safer than he would have been in foster care. But who was I kidding? I couldn't even keep myself safe. How could I protect him when I couldn't even protect myself?

Hope Doran

CAMP

Things progressed on. I did not want to be at the house, save my time with my brother. I just loved him too much to not be present. The softball practice I had been doing with Father dwindled down to nothing, as did my actual softball playing time. Mother was so obviously over me I was uncomfortable in her presence. I felt like a shell of a human, walking among the vibrant living. It was crushing.

Summer came around, and I was bored out of my mind. I had no sports, no close friends, no place I felt safe to just be present. It was excruciating, and my boredom cost me. My sullen attitude got me into trouble at every turn. With everything that had happened with the social workers, the parental units never hit me with the cutting board again, but they found other things to punish me with. The acres of land we lived on were heavy laden with weeds, and that became my new discipline. Mother spared no mercy. She would come out when I thought I was done and scrutinize my work, often telling me it wasn't good enough because fragments of weeds were left behind. It got to the point I would just sit outside all day, whittling away at the weeds to stay away from her, popping up to look productive when I could hear her heavy footsteps coming down the driveway.

I daydreamed about summer camps. The church youth had been talking about going to some of the many that were offered among the different local churches. I didn't even bother asking to go. I assumed the answer would be no. It was a week of fun that the other church kids would come back from, discussing the activities among themselves. In years past, I would listen from the fringes as my peers spoke of their experiences. I was always jealous of such talk that I was socially excluded from for lack of participation. My completion of Missionettes and the Honor Star celebration was my first camp experience. Now that I had that taste of youth camps, I wanted it even more.

Then, the most amazing thing happened. They let me go! There was really no fanfare to them telling me. It was more just a matter of fact, like I had been going for years. I was ecstatic! I was going with people I was developing friendships with at the new church. It was groundbreaking for me.

I packed everything I could think of that I might need. I loaded up with clothes, shoes, swimsuit, PJs, and toiletries. They were all shoved into a flimsy suitcase. I was so eager to escape my home I was practically giddy. The parental units dropped me off at the church, and us kiddos headed out in the church van.

Once we got settled into our camp cabins, we were able to do some exploring. I ventured out taking in the possible activities I could do. There was a massive swimming pool that I couldn't wait to get into. I trolled around a bit more, meeting other kids, chit chatting with them and walking on some of the hiking paths. It was odd, but I felt out of place. I had been in trouble so much at the house free time had become scarce. I didn't know what to do with myself, and soon began to wander around aimlessly.

I ran into a boy while out on my adventures. He was my height, with red hair and a freckled face. We struck up a conversation. I felt this strange tingling in my gut as we talked. I watched his mouth forming his conversation, mesmerized as I watched his lips. His eyes were very blue, and they lit up as we spoke about where we were from, how old we were, had we been there before, and so on. I didn't know it, but I was experiencing my first crush. We parted ways as the call back to the cabins rang through the summer air. There was a promise to meet up at dinner, and I walked away on cloud nine.

I floated through the rest of the day, barely taking in the cabin rules. I met the other girls as we stood in a circle, giving our names, where we were from, and something fun about ourselves. When it came to my turn, the first two were easily answered, but I fumbled on the last. I did not consider myself as fun. The best I could come up with was being a Missionettes Honor Star. I watched the faces of the girls around me. I knew I had come across as arrogant. So, with that I had become a boastful person to keep at arm's length. I discovered the learning curve for social niceties is sharp, and quickly regretted my disclosure.

In spite of the coolness among some of the cabin girls, I was still relieved to be there. The reprieve from the parental units was a gift, and there were a couple of girls who befriended me. I was grateful for the company. We would go from one church event to the other, Bible studies, church singing, group and private Bible time, and share time to discuss what we learned. All other time spilled out into the extracurricular activities like swimming, hiking, art or some other crafting class. Even in my social awkwardness, I had a wonderful time.

The week had almost come to a close. I had spent time with the boy, and we had so much fun together, meeting to eat, swim, or to hike. On one hike nearing the end of the week, he took my hand as we walked. I flushed immediately, and my hand became cold and clammy in his, but he didn't let go. I thought I might throw up as we walked. It was the most fascinating combination of feelings that I eagerly welcomed. We parted ways with a promise to meet at the pool for the last day's pool extravaganza.

I ran to the cabin to get myself ready. I pulled out my swimsuit and went to the bathroom to change. I pulled off my underwear and there it was. Aunt flow had come to town. It was not the first time I had my period, but as a new member into this level of womanhood, I was far from regular. I located a pad and went back to my bunk defeated. There would be no pool rendezvous with the boy... I was way too embarrassed to tell him I had started my period.

I was sulking on my bunk when the cabin counselor came into the cabin. She asked why I wasn't at the pool. I told her I started my period. Her response was "So what?" I looked at her puzzled and said, "I can't go into the pool, I'll bleed everywhere!" She looked at me puzzled and asked why I wouldn't wear a tampon. Mother had never given me the option of using a tampon. Pads had been the only things

I was told to use. I had no education on tampon use, or how in heaven's name that would keep my period from becoming public knowledge. There, in that cabin she verbally explained how a tampon worked and how to use it. She gave me the instructions and told me to use one of those, and I would be able to go swimming.

I didn't understand why Mother had not discussed this with me. It seemed simple enough. Once I positioned it in correctly (it did take a couple of tampons to figure that part out), I was good to go. I threw on my swimsuit, grabbed my towel, and hollered a thank you to the counselor as I blazed my way down to the pool.

The pool was amazing! I met the boy, and together we played water games with other kids. My secret safe, although I did check a couple of times to make sure I wasn't leaving a tell-tale-trail in my wake. We sat in the sun, dove into the pool, and splashed each other silly. I could not remember ever having felt so alive. It was a glorious day. By day's end, I had a week worth of sun on my body, people who liked me and a feeling of calmness that I seldom came across.

Then it was done. The following day was a bittersweet one. I had to return home. I was not looking forward to this, save being able to see my brother. I slowly packed my things, stealing away my memories in the recesses of my mind to pull from during the hard times I was most assured were coming. As I walked to the church van and dropped my things for loading, I felt someone come up behind me. It was him. He took my hand, and we ran into a group of trees, and there within the trees, with the sun sneaking through the leaves, Ricky gave me my first kiss.

The ride home I was on cloud nine. I could still feel his lips as if they had seared themselves to my own. It left me daydreaming the entire ride home. I knew he lived too far away, but it didn't stop my wandering thoughts. We pulled into the parking lot and my happiness must have been showing because Mother asked me what happened at camp. She rarely asked such things. I gave her assorted details as we drove home, but nothing of the real reasons for my happiness.

Later that night I needed more personal supplies. Not thinking much of it, I lightly asked Mother for tampons. She asked how I knew about tampons, and I told her the counselor had given me one so I could go swimming. I could tell immediately that was a mistake. Mother's scowl formed deep creases in her face as she contemplated what she would say. Having made her choice, she pierced me with her cold, blue eyes as she stood up from her chair. Her words cut into me as she flatly stated that I had lost my virginity because I had used a tampon. She continued with telling me my future husband would have no way of knowing if I was a virgin because I stuck a tampon up inside me.

I stood there in shock. It didn't make sense that the church camp counselor would have given me something that would destroy my virginity. Everything I was being taught in church stated that I needed to keep myself pure, to not have sex before I was married. Now Mother was telling me I had ruined myself.

    She followed that by saying if I was lucky, maybe I'd marry someone who didn't care that I wasn't a virgin. With that she retreated to the depths of her bathroom and returned with a box of tampons. She handed them to me as I stood trembling, sobbing in disbelief over what I had done to myself. I didn't want to take them from her, but she shoved them into my chest, forcing me to take them. I said I didn't want them, and she said that I might as well use them seeing as I already ruined myself. She walked off smugly. I was left standing there, alone, embarrassed, and mentally destroyed.

Hope Doran

VOLLEYBALL

The summer break was coming to a close. I would be starting high school. I had gone to orientation, which included information on club and sports activities that were available. They made it sound so exciting, and something that would look good on college applications. I wanted to give it a go. I had always been athletic and enjoyed volleyball in junior high PE class. I thought I would ask to try out for fall volleyball, and then softball in the spring.

I took the bus home and Mother asked how everything went. She had not been pleased to send me off alone, but I had reached an age where it was becoming inevitable. I cautiously told her things had gone well and included the idea of sports. She seemed receptive, so I asked if I could try out for volleyball.

It was a discussion that I thought went well. She asked how many days tryouts were, how I would get there and how I would manage my grades, which had been piss-poor in junior high school. I explained that tryouts started tomorrow and went most of the days for the next week. I offered that I could take the bus so I wouldn't impose on her. As far as my grades were concerned, I told her I had to have a minimum GPA to participate, so that would be a good incentive for me to work harder. She said, "okay." I was shocked and excited.

I proceeded to shuttle myself to and from home and school. The volleyball coach was beyond nice. I knew the basics of volleyball but didn't know a lot of play formations the other girls had been doing for some time. The coach took her time with me, breaking them down, moving me around the court to become familiar with the different play positions and the roles with them.

When I would get home, Mother would ask how things were going. I was surprised at her interest but welcomed the conversation. I would tell her the ups and downs of practicing and tryouts as well as any adventures during the bus ride home from town. At the time, I thought it was a bonding moment.

Before I knew it, tryouts were over. I had to wait until school began to find out if I made the team. I wandered through my days, wondering if I made the cut. Mother continued to be supportive, telling me I would find out soon enough. I grew impatient and excited for the start of school.

The first day of high school was an exciting one. I had a couple of classes with my dear friend, Cynthia. We had met the previous year in junior high. She was a lifeline for me, and I valued our time together, even if it was in class. We had become fast friends. She met me at the front of the school, and we went down to the gym to see the post. I looked over the list, and there, neatly typed was the JV Volleyball team list. My name was printed clear as day. I made the team.

I was so excited! The first day I was on cloud nine. It was amazing! The high school was even bigger than the junior high, and there were so many new faces to meet. I had come into my own, and the new kids enjoyed me. Cynthia was so sweet, and together we made a great set of friends, both to each other and to others. I was becoming more confident in who I was, despite my circumstances.

The bus ride home was a long one, but I didn't care. I couldn't wait to tell Mother I had made the team. We were supposed to start practice the following day, and we were given the schedule of practices and games. I was so proud of the fact I had made the team; I couldn't keep the smile off my face.

I jumped off the bus and ran up the driveway to the house. I had the schedule in my hand, ready to go over it with Mother. There were uniform costs and travel expenses, but the coach had said not to worry about it for any of the girls that had concerns over expenses. I thought I was a shoe in. All I needed was a signature from Mother to participate.

I charged up to the screen door, flinging it open. It slammed behind me as I looked for Mother. Not finding her, I assumed she was in her bedroom, which was strictly off limits. I was not even allowed to talk through the door. I sat patiently and waited for her to emerge. My fingers fondling the paper that proved I was good at something; I was worth something.

My wait was not too long. Mother emerged from what seemed to be a nap. Unable to contain my excitement, I ran up to her blurting "I made the team!" I excitedly shoved the schedule and information into her limp hands with a big smile plastered on my face. She looked at me, then at the paper, then back to me. She handed me the packet back and flatly said, "You can't play."

I froze. What do you mean I can't play? I asked. Repeating to her that I had made the team. She looked at me flatly and told me she let me try out because she didn't think I'd make the team. With that, she spun on her heels and retreated to her room. I was left alone, in shock. I let the paper slip from my fingers and fall to the floor. I somehow managed to get my shocked body to move and went to my room. Nothing was ever spoken about any high school sport again.

VINYL ON FIRE

The human construct of religion is so absurd. It seems humans are always contorting the Bible to say what they want it to say, to frame its words into something that serves their purpose. I had no idea of the depths of religion until the parental units were blindly immersed in the Pentecostal Christian faith. From that point on, if something didn't line up with what they thought the Bible said, it was sinful. I had to tread lightly in my goings on, even more so than before.

I had taken to cutting school, the last real power I had over my life. I went when I felt like it, cut when I didn't, and disconnected the landline when I got home so the parental units did not receive the notification calls. I had also befriended student aids in the office that would change my absence for me. It's fair to say I cut classes an obscene amount in my early high school years. It was my only available blatant 'fuck you' to the parental units, and I was liberal with it.

I had to plan out my time getting home carefully. Having cut the entire afternoon, I almost missed the only bus that would get me home at my regular time. I lugged my way up the driveway to see there were no cars there. I was instantly relieved. Assuming Mother had gone into town that meant I likely had the house to myself until Father got home.

I flung open the door, dropping my backpack on the floor. I grabbed a snack and got on the phone with Cynthia. She and I always spoke on the phone when I got home, and I didn't want her to wonder or worry about me if she called later. When we said our goodbyes, I disconnected the phone line from the jack just enough to be disengaged but look like it was still connected to the wall. With the phone ready for silence, I quickly became bored. I sauntered over to the radio receiver, and turned it on, switching it from its usual talk radio station to KDON. The music was top forty, something I rarely heard, but really enjoyed. Church music was the only music I was allowed to listen to save these scarce moments in time.

I swayed around the dining and living room, which was one big open space. I started humming to some songs I didn't know all the words to, but that shifted to jubilant singing with the ones I did. The music lightened my mood and was something I immensely enjoyed. I sang my sinning heart out, without a care for where that would land my soul.

A song came on the radio that was so popular, even I knew it word for word. I cranked up the radio way louder than what was ever approved, church music or not. I danced around the living room singing the lyrics to Stacey Q's "Two of Hearts." My heart felt free, as I grooved, danced, and jumped around the room singing the chorus full blast. I was gyrating around, lost in the music when something caught my attention.

I swung around to see Mother, standing there, staring at me in disbelief. I spun back, turning the large metal dial all the way down in one quick motion and turned back to her. The air was thick with silence. I looked outside and saw that she had parked the car high above the driveway, out of my line of vision coming up to the house. She had been there the whole time.

I turned back towards her. Mother just stood there, not saying anything. It was a stare off of sorts. It ended with her turning and retreating to the bedroom where she had been, without saying a word. I must have woken her when I turned up the volume so loud. In spite of being discovered, I returned the receiver to the talk show it was on before turning it off. I picked up my backpack, went to my room and awaited the arrival of Father and my discipline. It seemed any discipline I now received still had to include Father. I think it was a way of letting me sit in what had happened and work myself up with worry. Whatever the reason, I did dread the waiting.

When Father arrived, I could hear Mother hustling out to the van. I knew she would talk to him about my sinful actions. I sat and waited in my room. They both came in, and I could hear both of them moving around. They were collecting things, but I couldn't tell what. I went into the bathroom and opened the small sliding window, which gave me a slight view into their actions, and peeked outside.

My view was obstructed as I stared out past the cabinet, which was to the side of the bathroom window. I could barely see out past the porch screen door where they had gathered. It was music. I stared horrified as I watched them place 8tracks, cassettes, and their massive collection of vinyl records into a scattered pile on the ground.

When all was said and done, there was a mess of timeless music, The Beatles, Eagles, Fleetwood Mac, Johnny Cash, Rolling Stones, Aerosmith, Credence Clearwater, Lynyrd Skynyrd, Tom Petty, Journey, and Styx just to name a few of the hundreds of music artists we had in our home and vehicles. They were all piled high on top of one another reaching for the sky, like things cast off that no longer serve purpose for their owner, awaiting their fate. I saw Father retrieve a blowtorch from his seemingly endless stock of tools. It was then they called me out to join them.

Mother started with telling me the music before us was evil. She said Satan served no purpose in our house, and they were rebuking him out of our house, cleansing our house and me from the sin of secular music. She and Father prayed for forgiveness of my sinful ways. With that Father started the torch. I looked at her, contemplating asking why she did not ask forgiveness herself, seeing as she had provided and housed such an evil within our house all these years. Thinking better of it, I stayed silent.

Mother picked up the first album, holding it out toward Father. He passed the lit torch over the vinyl, and I watched as the heat of the flame warped and destroyed the record. I cried as the lines in the vinyl representing a song melted into oblivion as the heat bent the record into a useless, plastic wad. Mother let it fall from her hand, and it fell clattering its last breath onto the cement patio. I stood in silence as I watched piece after piece of my memories destroyed by narrow minded people who thought stripping music out of our lives would save me.

I mourned the loss of the music. It was a piece of me. It reminded me of the move out to California, time spent with Grandma, times where music kept me sane. That music even reminded me of a few of the favored moments with the parental units. All of it was gone with no remorse from either of them. I stood there while the parental units became gleeful in their destruction, praising God for setting me free from the sin of secular music. I watched them with disbelief as they bantered about how the flame looked like something evil that was trapped in its heat. The only thing I saw were two people lost in religious zealousness commenting over imaginary demons within a fiery torch as they destroyed a piece of me without caring about what they had done.

No music was ever allowed in the house for the rest of my youth. The receiver was relocated to an unknown location. I was not without my music though. A new way of listening to music through a Walkman had become more easily available. Although I was not allowed to have one, it seemed I was usually able to have a friend loan me theirs for the night. Cassette tapes were too pricey, but I was able to listen to some radio stations, and *Delilah After Dark* became a radio favorite. I would tuck in under my covers, only coming out for air when I was desperate, just to retreat under the covers in case they came in. I listened through the cheap foam headphones, letting the voices coming through them lull me to sleep. Music became my church, my refuge in its unbiased nature, and I attended daily.

Hope Doran

DEAR DIARY

It seems that at some point during our lives we are told to keep a diary. It could be for a plethora of reasons from having a hard time recalling daily events to processing trauma. Regardless of the reason, keeping a record of life events can be very healing and become a record of events we can reference later in life as needed.

At some point in my youth, I started keeping a diary. I was so full of anger, rage, and frustration I needed a release. It started as a requirement for a school assignment. Once the assignment ended, I just continued. It wasn't a daily thing, but I wrote in it often. I had concerns of the parental units finding my pages, but as time went on, I grew careless. My diary was full of everything. Moments of home life I hated, school troubles, things I had heard about other people at church or school, my own personal thoughts about things, crushes I had, and teenage daydreams about things I would do with the crushes I had. I was sexually passionate in my imagination, thinking the flaming hot pages were for my eyes only.

One crush was not completely unrequited. We had a new youth pastor in the new church (yes, yet another new church). He was in his early twenties, and to me, very handsome. I was smitten. I could not wait to go to the youth group and would go out of my way to talk with Lloyd. He was charming, charismatic, and friendly. We ended up hanging out at one point outside church.

Nothing ever happened that was sexual, although there was definitely flirting. My diary exploited those times, indulging in sexual fantasy with him. My young mind spared no fantasy; to the point my own sexually premature writing was arousing to me. I should have hidden the diary better.

Time went on and eventually Mother found purpose to ransack my room. I came home from school to see my things spread out on the dining room table. There were many things she found, but the one I couldn't take my eyes off was my diary. My stomach dropped. I felt faint. My fleeting hope that she hadn't read my diary was quickly crushed within her command to sit down. She had read it all. She dove into my writing without remorse. She consumed all my words, thoughts about her, Father, my anger towards them, my desire for something different, my crushes. She was livid over everything in it. I sat stiff, waiting for her to finish her tirade, crimson red with fury and embarrassment. The thought that a diary is private is a beautiful one, but only if that unwritten rule is honored. Mother never really honored anything I wanted.

Aside from being furious regarding my thoughts on her, school, and other choice entries, she also felt the need to read out loud my entries about Lloyd. I watched, as her anger was present as she read my most private, very sexual daydreams. She couldn't see the forest for the trees. I tried telling her they were fantasy, but she would not listen to me. She kept saying I ruined a good young man, and I should be utterly ashamed of myself for not acting like a Christian

Lady. I didn't understand how I ruined him, but suddenly feared for what she could do to him.

Her rage bled into the telephone as she called the pastor of the church. She told him of my diary, and the things I said about Lloyd. He asked to speak to me, and she shoved the phone into my hand. The pastor asked if he had had sex with me. I again said no, there was never any sexual activity. He said goodbye, and I handed the phone back to Mother.

When Mother was done on the phone, both the parental units told me I was grounded for everything with Lloyd as well as being ungrateful for what I had. Mother said I should take some time to write a hundred things I was grateful for in the family. She said I would be grounded for a month after I turned in the list. I don't recall how long I was grounded for.

And Lloyd? I don't know what ever happened to him. I was told he was dismissed as the youth pastor. Thanks to Mother, I felt like my ungodly ways ruined him, and I held that guilt for a number of years before I got old enough to realize that at my 14 years of age, I was just a child with a crush. It was his responsibility to be professional, and although nothing sexual or romantic occurred between us, a line was crossed as a pastor, and he was the one who crossed it.

As far as a diary goes, this is the closest thing to a diary that I have written since then. At least this time I write it wanting it to be read. I don't care if the parental units read it. This is my truth, which I kept quiet all these years to save an un-savable relationship with Mother. I write this because I want people to feel like they are not alone. I want to be a voice for people who are still trying to find their way through this way of life, to express they are not alone in their journey.

SPEAKING IN TONGUES

The church drenched our lives in its teachings and practices. The parental units were completely sold that this was the only way to be saved from certain damnation. They spared no expense in throwing me into any church activity that would save me from my sinful ways. I didn't mind though, it meant I was able to be away from them for periods of time, and frankly I enjoyed that time. Despite what they thought of me, I was trying to do the right thing for myself when it came to my immortal soul. Mother just never understood what was necessary for her, was not necessary for me. She saw Christianity as a one size fits all. I considered religion as a guide for life. I saw, even in my younger years, religion isn't perfect, nor should it claim that it is.

One time while at another church camp, there was a call to salvation. I raised my hand and went forward to accept my salvation, again. You see, even though I had a previous experience with turning my life over to Jesus, Mother had led me to believe that I had lost my salvation. I thought I had to ask the Lord to save me yet again. Lost were the teachings that the Lord loved everyone right where they were at. Instead, Mother's voice permeated the crevices of my mind, telling me I had lost favor with the Lord and needed to come back to him and hope he accepted me back into his flock. It was designed to be a highly emotional event, and that held true for me. Through ugly crying and sobs, I made a commitment to the Lord, to follow in his ways and be the best Christian I could be.

The camp pastor leading the service laid a hand on my forehead, and I began speaking in tongues. These strange words were coming out of my mouth, being voiced by me, but understood by no one. Even so, everyone around me became exuberant and we were all jumping around, praising God. I was excited, and moving forward, every time I prayed, I included this "prayer."

When I told her, Mother had told me that speaking in tongues was an outward sign of an inward commitment to God. She was very excited and happy about my newfound prayer language. She said it meant God has claimed me and that was visible to anyone who heard me pray in the unknown language.

This had all happened when I was in my younger years, but I had continued in the practice of speaking in tongues as I grew older. Mother grew concerned that my "prayer language" didn't grow and began to pick at me over that fact. She would say things to the effect of telling me my prayer language should grow as my relationship with God grows. She would say I needed to get myself right with God so my language would evolve. It got to the point I told her it had never grown, and she asked to pray over me. In her prayer, she asked that my prayer language reflect my growth in Christ, and if it was not from God, then it be gone from my memory.

Instantly it was gone. Could not recall it, didn't want to recall it. Mother panicked, telling me I should seek out my heart, renew my faith in the Lord and ask for a prayer language that was from the Holy Spirit. She said she was grateful she rebuked Satan from my heart, but obviously my walk with the Lord was not where it needed to be. I challenged her regarding prayer language being required for salvation. She scoffed at me, telling me although it was not required for salvation; it was required for spiritual growth. She accused me of being stagnant in my faith, in jeopardy of falling out of God's grace, and losing my salvation once again. I said okay, but only to end the discussion.

Years later she revisited this conversation with me by phone, telling me again that she had concerns for my spiritual health. I asked her why the Bible would tell me to know what it is I'm praying for, but then expect me to speak in tongues? I explained that for me, it didn't make sense to seek out speaking in tongues because I did not know what I was saying. I wanted to be concise in my prayer to God, and tongues had no place in my life because the language was unknown to me.

She sidestepped my question, not answering it, but trying instead to discuss the topic. I prodded further, asking again, "If I am talking in some other language, which I don't even understand, how do I know I am not asking or praying for some horrendous thing?" She repeated, "It's a language of God." I asked her, "How do you know? How do you know what YOU are praying is pure and from God?" She hung up on me. We never spoke about it again.

Hope Doran

FAMILY

In spite of moving closer to family by relocating to California years earlier, we were incredibly isolated from them. Mother had laid down the law for seeing Grandma, but for whatever reason, my aunt and uncle on my father's side were also rarely seen. Mother's brothers (at least one of them) were also living in California. I never did meet him or any of my cousins. To this day I'm not sure why. I often wondered why Mother never visited any siblings during my lifetime. It spoke to how she viewed family. However, I will say that Father always seemed to find ways to visit his brother and sister freely without the company of Mother.

In the earlier years of our lives in California we would visit my uncle and his wife frequently. I recall my uncle would often have us over to their beautiful house in Oakland. We would traverse into San Francisco for the day. They all seemed to get along well back then. During one of these visits, Father's wardrobe was discussed because he didn't have the most appropriate attire for interviews. Knowing the parental units were tight on money, my uncle offered several of his own suits to my father. I found the gesture to be a kind one, and Father went home with suits, shirts, ties, and even shoes on several occasions. It started with looking more professional for interviews, but Father benefited from uncle on another occasion, when Father wanted to look sharper for our church adventures.

Despite the kind gesture, I can't recall how many times I heard Mother rant about the suits. She made mention of it for years following the time Father was able to afford his own suits. By that time, they were solely for church functions. Father looked quite dapper in my young mind, but that didn't matter. Every time he donned one of the suites from uncle, she would comment on how worn they were, how out of date they were, or how ill-fitting they were. Even in my younger years I thought it was offensive, and didn't understand why she would be so ungrateful, and try to create the same ungratefulness in my father.

As I grew older, it seemed Mother's opinion never really improved regarding Father's family, although she seemed to respond most positively towards my father's sister. There were several conversations that I held with Mother regarding my father's brother, and for the life of me, I can't recall a single positive one. Sadly, her opinions towards my uncle tainted my views of him as well. It wasn't until adulthood that I realized that I didn't share her views, but by then, attitudes were well established, and all parties were comfortable with things as they were.

Before the establishment of cool attitudes, my uncle would often invite us out to do things with his wife, and later their child as well. There were several occasions we all hung out. They all held fond memories for me, and they were fun times. Everything seemed okay on these occasions, and I always waited for a shift in attitudes from Mother, but that shift never came.

There was one blustery winter season in my early teenage years when my uncle had invited us all up to a ski resort. I had never been skiing, and thought it sounded like tremendous fun. We hadn't seen a legitimate snowfall since we had moved from Illinois. I recall hearing the parental units discussing it at great length before declining the offer. My uncle then offered to have me come up with them for the snowy vacation. At that point I became very excited, thinking I would not only have a break from the house, but also be able to spend time with Father's family and learn how to ski. He even offered to pay the rental costs for the attire and equipment I would need.

The discussion about me going was brief. Mother didn't want him to pay for my trip and told me that she didn't trust me to be safe in the new sport as I was a bit of a daredevil. She also said because of my lack of fear, she didn't trust the family to keep me safe. I was upset. Mother had never let me do any sport aside from the recreational softball I had been allowed to play in my younger years, nor had I ever been injured from anything I had done.

The decision was unwarranted and unfair. There was no reason I shouldn't have been able to go. Mother let her attitude towards my uncle taint her decision. She told me she didn't want to accept any more "charity" from my uncle. I was crushed and thought it had more to do with her actual dislike for my uncle rather than anything to do with charity, but perhaps it was both. Perhaps it was that she wasn't invited with an offer to pay for her accommodations. I was always told by Mother to try new things, but then never allowed to do anything that would expand myself as an individual. I hungered for adventuring into new circles and pushing boundaries to get out of my comfort zone. I longed to better myself and connect with family. I felt she robbed me of a bonding moment with Father's family out of jealousy. I had always hoped for another opportunity with them, but that was the first, and last time anything of that magnitude was offered.

MOMMY DEAREST

I had become quite the avid reader in my younger years. Being isolated in the rural area of my small town in addition to being pretty much shunned until 8th grade attributed to my advanced reading level. I prized my reading skills, and welcomed all the locations, characters, and events that folded out page after page before my hungry eyes. I immersed myself in books as if they were a refuge. They were my safe haven to explore and experience friendships as I imagined myself within the unfolding stories. I would read about friendships, romances, mystery, fiction, non-fiction, murder, or death. As odd as it may sound, I learned a lot about what I wanted in life from my reading. I also learned a lot about who I wanted to be as a human. My ability and love for reading was very influential to me, and I am grateful for the lessons learned, even if they did fall within the pages of a fictional book.

Even with my newly acquired social acceptance, I still craved the sanctity of reading. It continued to allow me the opportunity to see the world through someone else's lens. Having gotten to the point in my life where I severely doubted that I would experience the world the way I wanted to, I immersed myself in the writer's vision of their own world they created. I longed to read about other people's successes, trials, and woes. It fortified the idea that I was not alone. Sometimes even offered the hope I would escape my own emotionally traumatic life.

There was a movie that had come out some time earlier. I never saw the movie, but it was also in book form. One of my friends said I might like it and handed me a copy. It was *Mommy Dearest*, written by Christina Crawford. I flipped through the pages, reading this or that and was immediately intrigued. I thanked her and went home.

Now, I had been careful about what Mother knew of my reading material. There had been numerous occasions where I had books that she most definitely did not approve of. Unfortunately, as I grew older, that became more frequent as I thirsted for the expansion of my small universe, whether it was through real life characters, fantasy, or erotica. Up until recently, her only trigger had been anything sexual in nature, although I did slip several Judy Bloom books past her, undetected.

Because *Mommy Dearest* did not seem to have sexual context in it, I did not think it would be a banned book, so I had it out with my other schoolbooks. When I was done with my homework, I grabbed the book and went to go outside to My Oak and read. On my way out, I passed Mother, who met my gaze before her eyes came to rest on the book. She snatched it out of my hands, asking where I got it. I explained that a friend had lent me the book. She responded by saying that was too bad as she tore the book in half. She flatly told me I wasn't allowed to read it.

I stared at her in shock. You see, I hadn't read enough of it to know there were vast similarities between Christina Crawford's experiences and my own. Mother touted it as simple inappropriate reading, but she had never done that with any other book that had not gained her approval. I grew to assume that she knew the story and felt it would hit too close to home. She really should have let me read it. It likely would have made me feel better about my situation. It was a story I could draw parallels from. I learned this as I discovered Christina Crawford's story later in life.

Hope Doran

CAT FOOD

Mother was always looking for new and innovative ways to discipline me. There was never a shortage of different ways this would occur. Occasionally, she would even discipline me because I completed my discipline wrong. There was a period of time when weeding was an ongoing discipline for the slightest wrongdoing on my part. The continuous weeding project was such a massive one that it left little room for other forms of discipline for the insurmountable number of things I had done wrong in her eyes. I think Mother enjoyed the boredom that engulfed me as I continued the weeding. It seemed that she got 2 forms of discipline in one.

To say I was sick of weeding would be an understatement. Living on acres of land provided ongoing weeding projects. I despised weeding. The tenacious Scotch Broom with its cute, vibrant yellow flowers against lush cascading billows of greenery had roots that went deep and would quickly change from weeds to small trees. I was expected to clear any given area with my bare hands. There was no mercy on Mother's end, and tree or weeds; I was expected to rid the area of everything before my punishment was deemed complete.

The days spent weeding were painful. Oftentimes I would end my days with sunburns, scratches, and blistered fingers with a full expectation to continue the next day until the disciplinary area was eradicated from the pesky weed. I continued in the process but would reach a point where my hands hurt too much to pull anymore. When this occurred, Mother would send me to bed without supper, stating I hadn't worked hard enough to eat anyways.

I would sit in my room, sullen and hungry, picking at the broken skin that had briefly held the blistered water bubbles before succumbing to the ragged surface of the branches leaving the tender skin below exposed and raw. It was never good enough; *I* was never good enough for her. I would cry in frustration and hunger, making sure my tears didn't fall onto the pink, raw, open skin as my hands lay limp in my lap. I was never going to be enough for her. It was the first time I actively thought about killing myself. I was so completely caught up in the idea that I wasn't wanted. I figured they wouldn't miss me, and no one else really would either.

I got up to get a knife from the kitchen. I snuck out through the bedroom door, seeing them sitting in the living room, watching TV. I easily got a knife and was back in my bedroom, undetected. I sat on the bed, pondering how I would cut. I figured being left-handed, I would strike my left wrist first because it would be strong enough after the cut to slice my right wrist. Drawing the tip of the blade across the delicate skin of my wrist, I tested the pressure before scratch turned to cut, and cut turned to wound. I put the knife down and watched the blood pool in the small divot of my wrist. The deep red turning vibrant as the blood ran down the sides, falling onto my lap. I felt as helpless as the blood looked as it fell, useless and still as it dropped onto my upper thigh, sliding down the sides of my leg coming to rest as the fabric of my comforter absorbed the red into its threads.

I realized something. I didn't think I wanted to die. I wanted my circumstance to die. I felt depressed, hopeless, lost, and lonely. Maybe if the circumstance were different, I would have still thought of ending my life, but in that moment, it was the clarity I needed to not finish what I started. I looked around my room, searching for a shift from desperation, and my gaze came to rest on a yellow bag of Meow Mix cat food, pondering its taste to humans. My hunger held few limits as I considered my next meal.

I wrapped my wrist in a washcloth and picked up the bag. I had never given a thought to feeding our cats, but now I sat and pondered feeding it to myself. I pulled out a handful, smelling it intently. It seemed okay. I tentatively took a kibble and put it in my mouth, chewing slowly, ready to revolt, and spew it out if it was too gross. It wasn't, so I kept eating until I wasn't hungry, and went to bed.

Mother never took notice of my wound, although she never took much notice of me in general. That was not the last time a blade would cross my skin, but for the moment, the desire to end my existence passed. After several times of having cat food for dinner, Mother caught me eating it. She shrugged, telling me if that's what I wanted to eat instead of just going to bed without supper, then I could have at it. Although she told me it was okay to eat, the cat food soon found its way to a different location in the house which was much more visible to her intent eyes.

Hope Doran

BORROWING

A fun component of friendship is the willingness and desire to share in everything. My circle of friends was very close, and we would share everything from makeup, to clothes, to food. Nothing was off limits. We traded everything and had fun doing it. There were several lunch periods where wardrobes were planned for the week, mascara was offered for a touch up, or a brush borrowed for some flyaway hair.

I don't have many fond memories of school but sitting on the front steps of the high school, sharing in plans, gossiping about one silliness or another, sharing food and laughs are all favored memories of mine. Aside from my brother, Cynthia was my favorite person, and I couldn't wait to share lunch with her. Even when I cut class, I came back to spend time with her.

A memory we laughed about for years was the one and only time I convinced her to cut class with me. We had walked to the local outdoor mall and were perusing the local merchants when her uncle spotted us. He made a very big deal out of the fact that he saw her outside of school before he walked off. She was so terrified he would share his discovery with her dad, but he never did, or if he did it was a rare moment when her dad let it slide. We were relieved, but I never talked her into cutting school again.

With not being in school like I should have been, borrowing clothes was hard to do because I couldn't always get clothes back to people when they wanted them returned. I could always borrow from Cynthia because we made time for each other. She had a super cute denim skirt that was acid washed, sat below mid-calf at the hem and had a modest slit up to the back to my knees. I was going to a get together at Mother's best friend's house and Cynthia loaned it to me for the weekend.

Saturday came and I donned the skirt, paired with a cute white shirt and some flat shoes. I felt cute, and Mother even said I looked nice. I beamed, having garnered some approval from her. We readied the house for our departure, with me in and out, loading things into the car. When we were all loaded up, we set out, and headed down the mountain.

As usual, it was a long ride into town, but at least it was a comfortable silence. My brother and I played in the back seat as Mother and Father talked easily between each other. Before we knew it, we were tooling down Highway 1, towards Capitola. A few more minutes of travel, and we arrived. We all disembarked and followed Mother to the front door as she smiled broadly for her friend. She always enjoyed visiting her best friend. I enjoyed these visits as well because the visits usually put her in good spirits.

We went into the cluttered house, and I made my usual way to the living room with my brother in my arms. The adults were all in the dining room when I got up to get one of John's toys that he had thrown (one of his favorite pastimes with me). As I picked it up, I turned to see Mother and her friend staring at me. I nervously asked what was wrong.

Mother came over to me, grabbing my arm tightly. She spun me around enough to look at my backside before flinging me back around to face her. She demanded to know where I got the skirt. I told her I borrowed it. She asked if I borrowed it from a whore because that's what I looked like. Shocked, I looked past her to see her friend nodding in approval, noting to myself, no wonder they're best friends. I wondered if Mother's friend had said something about my skirt being inappropriate because Mother had seen me earlier. Perhaps Mother didn't mind my skirt originally, but once her friend said something, she needed to act like she hadn't noticed the slit.

Mother turned to her friend apologizing for my lewd clothing. The response was to get me something appropriate from her daughter's wardrobe. I was given pants that were too big, so I spent the entire day trying not to have my ass hanging out as the pants kept slipping down to my hips (definitely not appropriate)! Every time Mother commented in shock over the skirt, I asked why I could wear a skirt as short as the slit went but got in trouble for the skirt I wore. The repeated question pissed her off, and I knew I'd pay for it later, but it was a legitimate question. I could see the fury mounting in her eyes, and I didn't care.

In the throes of my seeming inappropriate behavior and apparel, conversation between the two women shifted. That day was the first time I heard of Bethel Baptist Academy. Mother's friend regaled her with a story of conversion she witnessed from someone else. The story spoke of a ridged school in Mississippi which turned around a wayward boy who was headed to hell in a hand basket. He was not living a godly life. She said he had immersed himself in drugs and highly inappropriate sexual behaviors, but with the school's help, he was now living a godly life and was preparing to join the military. Mother was intrigued. I was bored. Mississippi was, I thought, too far away. Mother would never consider it. I shoved their conversation into the recesses of my mind.

Later, I got yelled at. Mother was on fire with anger. She said she was disgusted by my decision to wear the skirt and told me I looked like a harlot in it. Mother forbade me from borrowing clothes from anyone ever again. She said I humiliated her in front of her friend, who said Mother had no control over me, and that had embarrassed her. I listened to her rant, knowing by this time that I should just be quiet. When she was done, I choked out a lie and told her I was sorry and went to bed, grounded yet again for the crime of wearing a modest skirt with a 'sinful' slit in it that Mother had approved, and even complimented before I had left the house.

Another mistake I made was borrowing makeup from my friends. At 14 years of age, I was only allowed a pale blush and light pink lipstick. Mother refused to let me wear anything else. I would see my friends at school donning shimmering shades of blue, gray and purple hues upon their eyelids. Their eyes framed with jet-black mascara, and matching eyeliner making their eyes pop. I was so jealous of these girls as I wore what I, and other girls considered childish makeup in an attempt to fit in. It made me feel like a misfit. The looks from some of the girls let me know they shared my feelings.

I had enough of Mother's conversations about being a whore. Makeup did not make someone a whore, and I tired of Mother's rhetoric. I started borrowing makeup to put on once I got to school. I always arrived early and would transform myself within the shadows of the dimly lit bathroom. I learned early that eyeliner under the eyes was not a good idea, because it was too hard to erase in between the eyelashes at the end of the day. I would repeatedly get yelled at by Mother when I got home. She would meet me at the door, evaluating my face for any traces of what she considered whorish makeup that she liked to yell at me for.

One time when I came home with the remnants of makeup on my face, Mother slammed me down into the chair and told me to wait for her. She came out a short time later with half her face covered. She showed me the first side, which was very modest makeup, in pink and slight brown hues, and stated this was appropriate makeup. She then showed me the other, heavy-laden side, caked with makeup. I stifled a laugh, because I knew she did that because that's what she thought I looked like. She then asked me which side looked better. It was easy to tell her the light makeup side, because the other side looked like shit. Convinced I had learned my lesson, she dismissed me. What I learned was how to avoid her ridicule over makeup. I moved my PE class to the last period of the day and took swimming. Between the chlorine and shower after, I was

assured to be squeaky clean by the time I got home to
Mother's scrutiny with no traces of any makeup on my face.

CYNTHIA

Let me backtrack and tell you about Cynthia, it all started with a school lunch. Cynthia was new to the junior high school and looked how I felt. I was bitter over being held back in my 8th grade year. Mother said my grades weren't good enough to advance to high school. She battled the school board to have me withheld for another year of 8th grade. She won, and I stayed. I was mortified as I watched my peers graduate and advance into high school.

Without knowing each other's history, Cynthia and I ate lunch together, and a friendship was forged. Things came easily between us, and it was comforting to have the companionship. She was my first best friend. Not that I didn't have other friends at this point, but we were each other's best friends. I will go to my grave being thankful for her.

We commiserated on our lives, both coming from less-than-ideal situations (her story is hers to tell). It bonded us even tighter. Soon we were spending all our free time together, as we grew in friendship we sought out more time to have. There were classes shared, lunches where we shared our dreams of cars we would own. Hers, a classic yellow Volkswagen Karmann Ghia, and me, an old blue Ford Mustang. We would talk about boys we liked, school dramas that we had heard, or had somehow become entangled in, and the general plights of being teenagers. Day in, day out, I found myself looking forward to her company. Mother took a shine to Cynthia, so we were able to share time together outside school. We were thrilled. She was my strongest refuge for decades.

When we got into high school, our interests varied. That, and she was allowed to do activities like band class. I was always so jealous of her. The fun thing was that it expanded our friend base, and oftentimes there were about 15 of us kids piled onto the front steps of the high school, sometimes spilling out onto the grass during lunch hour. Through all of it Cynthia and I were always by each other's side.

The thing with large groups of friendships, sometimes they don't always go so smoothly. People connect and pull others in different directions as other friendships strengthen. Within the larger group, there was a group of 5 of us that initially connected and built a tight little unit of powerful bonds. We were content and happy sharing in this thing called friendship and thought we would be solid friends for a long time to come.

Unfortunately, jealousy is a massive beast. I had grown close to one of the girls in the group and started spending time with her as well. We became closer, as she and Cynthia became more divided. The divide affected all 5 of us, but mostly Cynthia and I. Cynthia and I remained strong, but the divide hurt us both. It got to the point I felt torn over who I would spend lunch with, wanting them both as friends and not understanding why we couldn't all be friends. I tried incessantly to create the same safe space we had all grown so comfortable in, but in the end, it was just no longer available.

At one point Mother overheard a conversation I had on the phone, and asked what was going on. I reluctantly told her that my friend had given me an ultimatum telling me I needed to choose either her, or Cynthia. The friend had said there wasn't room for both of them and if I didn't choose her, she would consider me as dead to her. Mother listened to me and when I finished flatly told me to choose Cynthia. I asked for advice on how to keep them both as friends, but she again told me to choose Cynthia.

It stung to not have any additional tools to navigate this new part of my life. Friendships had been so scarce for me, it seemed there should be a way to work things out for everybody, but without a whole lot of experience in the area of networking friendships, I chose the one that had been truest to me, the one who never gave an ultimatum, the one who, in spite of being hurt by the addition of this friendship, still chose me. I chose Cynthia. All these years later, if I had to do it all again, I would still choose her.

We were steadfast in our friendship and inseparable. I still remember her first car, an old green Pinto. I took a photo of her wearing an Amy Grant tee shirt, her face beaming with pride, the keys clutched tightly in her hand. I still have it to this day, along with so many others. She was the first of us to get a car, and we were all envious of her. There were other events, she went to prom, and she looked amazing. I wasn't allowed to go but was so glad she could. Later, when I was sent to Mississippi (more on that later),

Cynthia was one of two people that went directly to Mother and asked where I was, and the only one who remained my friend when I returned.

We spent decades in friendship. I wouldn't have traded her for anything. She and I have woven a lifetime of love and friendship around us. People should be so lucky to have had a friendship such as ours.

DOOMS DAY

Good Lord, if there was ever a recurring theme spilling out of Mother's tart mouth, it was the second coming of Christ. She never wasted an opportunity to tell me the Lord was coming back. I would often see her looking out from the large living room window, so intent in the expanse of clouds and sky. She held an almost peaceful look as she explored and processed what her eyes received, and there was softness to her when that occurred.

One time she caught me watching her. She told me she just knew the Lord was coming back soon, and stated she could feel it in her bones. She spoke with true excitement as she disclosed that she had a vision, and in it she watched the return of Christ from the very window I was facing. She finished her words, and returned her gaze to the sky, her eyes welling up with tears of gratitude over the inevitable return of Christ. It was almost eerie watching her in her trance-like state, so I retreated to my room.

Ever since my brother was born, she would talk incessantly about the return of Christ, the doom days leading up to Christ's coming, and how all the sinners who had not repented and made themselves right with the Lord would suffer dearly. Always sure to end with how sinful I was in my ways, and how that was reflected on her and Father. She said if I loved them, I would make myself right with the Lord. In hindsight, I think it was suggested to further instill fear in me, and the hope I would make right what were my sinful ways in her eyes rather than in the Lord's.

Well, her persistence worked, but not the way she had intended. I became so fearful of the return of Christ; it terrified me rather than excited me. I knew my own path with Christ was rocky, but also knew I was forgiven for my sins. After all, that's what the Bible said. Mother liked to twist it into a situation where there might be take-backs to my salvation. She would tell me that even though I had asked the Lord into my heart, if I lived a sinful life, the Lord would retract my salvation, and I would go to hell. It was a huge mind-fuck. I felt that God would either take me just as I was, or I'd be going to hell. In essence, if it was too late for me, then it was just too late. I knew I was a sinner, but I had tried to live as best as I could in those moments. Mother made it so I lived in constant fear of not being good enough for God. The good Lord certainly already knew I wasn't good enough for Mother.

But interestingly, despite my very real fear of what would happen to me, I worried more about what might happen to any future children I had. I gave a lot of thought to my brother going through Mother's biblical trials, and worried constantly for him. Being almost 16 at the time I was also giving thought to any future children I may have. I wasn't pregnant, but I pondered the situation and debated if I wanted to have children only to watch them endure the horrible atrocities Mother spoke so often about.

I also worried about my brother being tortured in Mother's warped rendition of the coming of Christ. The thought of him or any children dealing with this level of fear truly terrified me. It didn't seem right to have children when Mother was so certain the end times were right around the corner. I was angry with Mother for having my brother knowing in her mind that all of this was going to happen, knowing he would have to endure such terror. The more thought I gave to it, the less and less I wanted my own children, and the more I worried for John.

One time, we were driving into town and Mother made mention of the end times, and how excited she was for Christ's return and the rapture. I told her I was worried about the trials of faith that she had said were one of the markers for Christ's return. I told her there was no way I wanted to ever have children and force them into the foreseeable future of doom, at least as portrayed by Mother.

Mother was aghast that I had said such a thing. She asked why I wouldn't want to birth warriors for Christ. She was literally angry with me. I said I didn't think it was fair to bring children into a world that was on the brink of disaster. I said it seemed irresponsible for me to do so, and even said I was fearful for my brother. She regaled me with some candy-coated bullshit that the believers, and those who chose to honor, obey, and follow the words of Christ wouldn't have it that bad. She said if they were steadfast in their faith, that God would protect them. My only thought was that I never felt like God was protecting me, and we weren't even in the end times yet. I kept that thought to myself, certain she would have said something about my sinful ways blocking my faith in God's protection.

As if she heard my thoughts, Mother switched tactics, telling me that I should be concerned for my spiritual well-being if I didn't have the confidence to believe I would have Christ like children. I again told her it had nothing to do with my faith, but rather fear for what my children may go through. She said I should have enough faith in God to be able to raise them as followers in God. It made me wonder how she felt about her own salvation having had me, given her constant barraging of all my sinful ways.

Time went on and Christ did not return. The parental units moved out of the house Mother was so certain she would witness Christ's return from, and I grew less fearful. With all my life events with Mother, it was amazing how much I still believed her, and how much the indoctrination of her beliefs instilled crippling fear in me. She really was a masterful manipulator. However, the death of her religious vision of Christ's return, which she had held on to so confidently, was the first major breakdown of religion for me. I saw her vision of Christ's return disintegrate into thin air. Her religious armor that she clung to and took so much pride in failed before my eyes. The obliteration of her vision gave me hope in the future for my brother, and myself.

SNEAKING OUT

The prison that held me under the pretense of being home was stifling. With skipping school being my only way to say fuck you, I was constantly grounded. In being grounded, that meant school to home, church with them and nothing else. I settled in and called it good. It didn't matter if I had done better. Making the volleyball team to be told by Mother I couldn't play had taught me that there was no point in trying to do better, because it would never be good enough. I was never, ever going to be good enough.

Living in the Santa Cruz Mountains meant I was very isolated. I relied on busses or friends to get me home when I decided to sneak out of the house. It was easy enough for a while, but then the bus schedule changed, and I relied more on friends. It was risky, but Mother had not given me a reason to care. I snuck out of the house frequently, just to breathe. I needed to know there was room for me in the world beyond my current circumstance. I needed to see that I could fit outside the space that Mother had bound me to so tightly that I could scarcely breath, let alone grow.

One night I had decided to escape and go to a party in Santa Cruz. I had a friend who lived in the mountains that told me he would pick me up and take me back when the party was done. I staged my room as if I was sleeping and slipped out the door from my room onto the porch. From there, I escaped into the night like I had so many times before. I ran down to the road, met my friend, and we drove off into the night.

We arrived at the party and went off to our own groups of friends. The thing of it is, I wasn't a partier. I just wanted to be out. I wanted to feel free, to breath, to imagine a life beyond what I was currently living. I wandered around the house, watching the surrounding youth grow more and more inebriated as I continued to carry around the first drink I'd been given hours earlier. The night grew late, and I began to worry for my safety. I navigated my way around the house as boys became handsy with me whispering drunken wet words in my ear as they tried to pull me off into some darkened corner of a room. I slid out of another grasp as I found my friend.

I asked if he would take me home. He looked at me through glassy, half open eyes and said no. I could tell from looking at him he was very drunk and even I knew I was safer facing the wrath of Mother than a car ride up the winding roads of Bonny Doon with him. He gave me forty dollars and told me to take a cab as he sucked on a beer. I pushed back the tears of fear, took the money, and looked for a phone.

Keep in mind; this is back in the pre-cellphone days. I hunted around for some time before locating a phone. I realized I didn't know the address to where I was. I sat on the phone as I hollered to the kids around me, asking for the address. Unsuccessful, I breathed into the phone, asking if they would wait for me to look outside. They must have heard the panic in my voice, because I heard a reluctant yes from the receiver. I ran outside, down the street for the street name, ran back, frantically looking for the house number before running back inside, hoping the receiver was still off the phone.

    I waited outside for the yellow taxi. I had the money clutched tightly in my fist as I watched the sky beginning to show the slightest hint of dawn. I knew Father woke up at 7 am, and at 6:14 in the morning I was working off borrowed time as I slid into the backseat of the taxi. I watched as we headed towards home, taking note of how incredibly quick the meter was rolling closer and closer to my forty-dollar max. When it hit 39, I asked the driver to stop. We were in the middle of nowhere. It was obvious I was not to my destination. I handed the driver the forty dollars and went to get out of the car. Internally hoping I could sneak into the house after Father left for work. The driver asked me how much further to my house. I told him between 2 and 3 miles. He told me to stay in the taxi and he took me to my destination, telling me I should be more careful because I might not be so lucky next time. I thanked him, knowing he was right, and was still pondering his words as I slipped into my bedroom undetected.

    I wasn't so lucky all the time. The last time I snuck out of the house as a minor was to meet my boyfriend. I snuck out, running down the road to meet him in his hip little red car. We sat down the road from my driveway, just talking, eager to spend time together more than anything sexual. I sat in the passenger seat, facing him as we talked. From the corner of my eye, I saw a light exit from what I suspected was my driveway. The headlights shown down towards us before retreating into the driveway, pulling out to go the other direction.

Knowing I was discovered, I said goodbye and walked back up the road to the house. I went in the way I came, in case I was wrong, but Mother was there in my bedroom waiting. She asked me where I was, and I told her. She did not believe me, accusing me of whoring around. Even after I told her I saw Father's car lights, she called me a whore and left me alone in my room.

The silence over the matter in the following days was brutal. Conversation was scarce except for one interaction about the school in Mississippi. I had been wrong. Mississippi was not too far away for Mother to send me. The parental units showed me a brochure, telling me if I didn't want to live by the rules, they would send me off in the hopes of saving my soul. I told Mother I would adhere to their rules, and that was the end of the conversation. I mended my ways, going to school, coming home right after, and doing all the things I was supposed to. I was finally scared enough to pay attention.

It was the Friday before spring break. I was supposed to meet briefly with my boyfriend after school, but we missed each other. I got on the school bus, bummed I didn't get to see him one last time before the long week of school vacation. As the bus ascended into the windy turns, there was a small red car that was speeding behind us, closing the distance with quick precision around the weaving road. Once it caught up to us, I realized it was him. On a straightaway he pulled up along the side of the bus, honking his horn and waving at me as he drove. I felt so special. It was like something out of a movie. At the next stop, he jumped out of the car, his blond hair in his face as it so often was, ran up to my window and gave me flowers and a card. He told me he would call me over the spring break. He flashed his sweet sideways smile, folded his 6'3" frame into his tiny car and sped off.

That was the last time I saw Aaron. I heard from Mother he was the other person who inquired as to my whereabouts when I was gone to Mississippi. She did tell me she was not kind to him, accusing him of behaving in unchristian ways with me, jeopardizing my salvation, asking him how he could live with himself. She had said she was unkind, but when she told me the story, I could tell she was heinous and awful towards him. It made me feel bad because he was nothing but kind and respectful to me. He saw my situation, and I think was happy to give me a safe haven, even if it was brief.

Hope Doran

THE LENGTHS MOTHER WOULD GO TO

Mother gave me the news, her father, my grandfather, was dying. I hadn't seen him since before we moved out to California. She said he missed me dearly and wanted to see me before he passed away. Mother said she was going to attempt to work things out so I could go. She busied herself with making plans to visit him one last time over spring break. She confirmed I was to go with her, so I could see him one last time, just as he had wished for. I was sad to hear he was dying, but excited over the trip. It would be my first time flying.

Mother had me pack. Grandfather lived in Florida, so I packed shorts, tank tops, pants, and a bathing suit for the spring weather. Mother came in to inspect my packing. It did not meet with her approval, and she pulled out almost everything I had packed, replacing them with skirts, tee shirts, and sweaters. I told her I didn't want to wear those, but she insisted, telling me she wanted my grandfather to see me dressing modestly. I reluctantly complied, thinking it was weird because my clothes were not scandalous.

Father helped us load everything into the car before taking us to the airport. There, we said our goodbyes and boarded the airplane. I was nervous about flying, but Mother said it would be fine. The stewardesses went through the safety precautions, and before I knew it, we were in the air. I was mesmerized looking out the window, and watched the world as it passed by below us, like small, miniscule objects, silent and trivial in their existence.

We glided through the air. I was jumpy with the turbulence, not really knowing what to expect, but as I watched the others on the plane, there seemed to be no concerns, so I settled back. Flying wasn't nearly as exciting as I thought it would be, and I grew bored. I asked Mother for the ticket to look at. She hesitantly handed hers to me. I asked where mine was, and she mumbled something about it being packed away.

For the first time since the discussion of the trip had begun, I was wary. There was something about Mother that was more off than usual. I had learned to read her pretty well. It had become a necessity. I held her ticket in my clammy hands as I pondered it. I had watched her during the boarding process, and I knew she had to have both tickets accessible for me to get on the plane in the first place. My heartbeat faster as I started to take in the information. The ticket was to Alabama.

I looked at Mother, only to find her watching me. She knew I'd see it. I stammered out our landing location, questioning her while looking intently for any sign of faltering. She looked at the ticket, looked at me and calmly told me it was called a layover, and there would be another flight to Florida from Alabama. She was so calm about the whole thing, but I knew better. My heart was exploding in my chest. I was very aware that Alabama bordered

Mississippi, and her threat to dispose of me there weighed heavy on my mind for the remainder of the flight.

Once we landed, we walked through the airport. Mother seemed to be looking for something, so when she told me to sit down, I didn't question. I assumed she was looking for the next flight. I busied myself with watching her fade into the crowd and eyeing the other people bustling about. I should have been paying more attention.

I met the long slim fingers before anything else of Brother Owens. His fingers dug into my shoulder, and when I resisted, he switched from a stern to vice grip, digging into my clavicle. I almost passed out as I sought to evacuate myself from him, screaming, looking for Mother, only to find her watching the whole thing with massive intent. She made no attempt to intervene. I tried yelling, but Brother Owens' grip turned into such pain that it took everything just to stay conscious. He led me out of the airport. Mother was in tow with the luggage that she had gone to retrieve. The beady eyes of Brother Owens challenged any curious onlookers. No one intervened.

Brother Owens ushered me into an old, crusty sedan. Opening the door, he flung me in and slammed the door behind me. Like a trapped animal I lunged for the door handle, seeking any escape I could find. My hands met with a smooth door, save a hole where the handle to freedom had been removed to prevent my escape. The window crank was also gone. Mother slid into the passenger seat and Brother Owens took the wheel and we exited the airport, on our way to Lucedale, Mississippi.

I spared no words towards either of them as he drove. However, I was focused on years of pent-up rage towards Mother. I kicked the back of her seat, calling her a fucking bitch and a liar, telling her how much I hated her. Brother Owens calmly told me to shut up, or I would regret it deeply. He was so utterly sinister, I stopped talking for the rest of the ride. It could have been a Sunday drive with two friends the way he and Mother were conversing in the front seats as I took in every part of the drive that I could, fully intent on escaping at my first available opportunity. I noted the mileage on the car, off-ramps, and street signs, all in an attempt to plot an escape from an unknown prison. I quite literally wanted to claw, kick, strangle, and punch Mother with every passing breath.

I fixated on my hate towards her. I wanted her to wear every beating, every nasty thing she said, every dismissal of talent, every denial of life, every bone crushing lie, every heart-breaking refusal of love, every hate she had put into me, all of it. Instead, she sat making conversation with a total stranger as if I wasn't her caged daughter in the backseat of his car, awaiting my true fate after she was gone. It was highly symbolic of what I meant to her, but I wouldn't see that until years later, while writing this book.

When we arrived at Bethel, I was a little surprised. We drove into a long driveway that opened to a pretty, white, massive colonial style house. The surprise of its appearance did not destroy my desire for escape, and I waited at the door, crouched, and ready to lunge. Brother Owens was no rookie though. In one swift move he opened the door filling its frame, taking hold of me even as I tried to slide out from under his lanky, boney frame, and run. He twisted my arm behind me as he pulled me out of the car. I should have yelled out in pain, but all I saw was red fury. He forcefully escorted me into a small office with a huge wooden desk. There was one chair at each end. Brother Owens sat me down to face a new enemy, Brother Fountain at the other end. Mother stood awkwardly to the side, refusing to look at me as my eyes burned into her, wishing she was dead for lying to me, for putting me in Bethel, for not realizing I was a child of her own creation with all her hate, manipulation, and lack of love.

Brother Fountain was a stubby excuse of a man. It was immediately obvious that he spent an entire lifetime trying to compensate for it. He spoke in a clear level tone as he introduced himself. I looked at him observing who he really was. His eyes flashed to fury as he ordered me to cast my gaze down, telling me women had no place admiring a man or looking a man directly in their eyes. I scoffed at the suggestion that I would be admiring him. My chuckle was not well received, and when I looked at Mother, she had cast her gaze down as well.

Undeterred, Brother Fountain continued with the protocol for the school, he looked at the photo Mother had submitted of me, then looked at me saying I was much prettier than my photo. I mumbled something and was scorched again with his words of how women were not to speak to men unless given permission to do so. He told me that even in conversation, I was to never look a man directly in the eyes or respond directly to him unless I had been given permission to do so. He continued with stating women were not equal to men in any way, and therefore did not deserve to be treated as equals. He stated harlots behaved in such brazen and sexual ways, and he would not allow such behavior in his school. He informed me that "Proverbs Chapter 7" would be the first chapter of the Bible that I would memorize in an attempt to cast out my slutty spirit, lest I destroy a godly man with my sexual ways.

I scoffed at him again. His beady eyes bored into my burning face as he leaned his short frame over his massive desk, pointed a stubby fat finger at me, and said he would break my spirit if it were the last thing he did. Fresh on my pent-up rage towards Mother, I leaned over my half of the desk, looked him square in the eye and said, "Try."

I suspect I was bolder than he had prepared himself for. He sat back in the chair, looked at Mother, then me, and told me to say my goodbyes. I looked Mother dead in the eyes and said, "I hate you." With that, my lying, manipulative, narcissistic mother exited the office, off to her dying father. She left me there after hearing they used "unusual methods" for punishment. She left; even after hearing they use excessive corporal punishment in the hopes of saving my soul. She left with a look of relief on her face as she passed me by, leaving me with monsters to do with me what they would. Her exit was swift, leaving a massive hole in my heart that never healed.

My first days there were as one would suspect, horrendous. After Mother left, I was dismissed, and taken to be strip searched by some creampuff, pouty teenaged girl who acted like she was the best thing since sliced bread. In spite of her larger body, she spared no expense over ridiculing mine, telling me that my athletic frame was all wrong and my thighs were disgusting. I stood in front of her, naked as the day I was born and told her she was a disgusting bitch. For that I spent the rest of the afternoon on all fours, picking lint off the pristine carpet until it was time for dinner. She said my place was on the floor, and that I wasn't worthy of the gift of standing.

I thought dinner would be a relief. Nothing could be further from the truth. Men and boys came first for everything, so they ate dinner first. We girls got the "privilege" of serving them, to the point where we were responsible for setting up their meal, serving them, and cleaning up after them before finally proceeding with our own meal and subsequent cleanup.

While our own cleanup was underway, I was tasked with sitting on the greasy kitchen floor scouring a stainless-steel pot with a steel wool pad. I was told to transform the blackened pot to its former presentation, making it shine as if it were brand new. I set to my task as girls kicked me around in their own hustle to not be assigned my fate. I barely noticed the hundreds of micro-cuts on my hands as a result of the scouring pad. I observed my surroundings, the other girls, and the ever-present Brother Owens, walking through the kitchen, the girls parting ways, making a path for him as if he were Moses parting the Red Sea, wordlessly judging as he scrutinized each of us. I could see he felt powerful, and it annoyed me. I met his gaze and was quickly swatted on the arm with his ever-present switch. "You were told to never look a man in the eyes" he retorted as I rubbed my stinging arm. For the first time since I arrived, I cried.

We were all in bed by 8 pm. I laid in the top bunk, pondering escape. In my short time there I had already seen a girl get "licks" for talking to another girl. I watched as she was told to bend over, grab her ankles, and wait for Brother Owens to swat her with a switch on her ass. I was immediately reminded of my own encounters with such discipline, and it left my stomach sour as I tried not to vomit. I wanted to formulate a plan of escape, but I couldn't focus. In spite of my unfamiliar surroundings, the emotional impact of the day had exhausted me, and I fell into a fitful sleep.

The girl I was told would be watching me to make sure I didn't escape woke me up in the dark of night. She told me to get dressed as she threw clothes in my direction. She proceeded to hiss at me to hurry, and not wake the other girls as I groggily got out of bed and went into the bathroom. She watched as I changed, telling me I was too slow. When I asked what time it was, I was told time didn't matter anymore. When I was dressed, she escorted me to the girl's schoolroom, where Brother Fountain awaited my arrival.

He ushered me into the adjoining bathroom. There I took inventory of several toilets, naked of their stall walls which would have provided privacy. There was a stale stench to the air, and I struggled to not make a face as he lifted the lids to the toilets, and the ripe smell of fermented urine and feces accosted my sense of smell. The facility has obviously not been working for some time, yet people had continued to use the toilets as if they did. The toilets were filled to the brim, and housed urine so fermented it was the color of caramel. The feces had been turned to thick sludge covering the bottom of the toilets like fine silt at the bottom of a lake. I looked at Brother Fountain confused as to why we were there.

He handed me 2 plastic bags. They were bread bags that you would find holding loaves in a grocery store. I took the bags confused, still not understanding why we were there. He smirked and told me to clean the toilets. I stared at him in disbelief, and he retrieved a switch from the back of his boot and said, "Clean these toilets," as he pointed with the switch in their direction. "I want them to shine like the return of Christ when you're done." I stared at him in disbelief, but his sadistic smirk told me he meant what he said.

I surmised that the bags were meant for me to use as a feeble attempt to protect my hands from the thick liquid. Nevertheless, I tied a knot at the top of the bag and shimmied my hands in as best I could. He had given me a bucket to transfer the vile liquid and walk it over to the muck room at the kitchen across from the school and dump it down the drain. I dove my hands into the murky liquid, and the stench rocked me so hard I vomited into the toilet.

I was in that position for some time as the stench and the feeling of the gooey texture against my hands paralyzed me, save the retching of my body. My watcher, overcome by the smells and sights, began vomiting herself and was told to wait outside. Alone with him in the room, I had a moment of clarity. This was his play. This is what he intended to break my pride, my spirit. This was his end game. Armed with this belief, I gained the mindset of a warrior. I choked back the bile, refusing to hurl anymore, and began my task in earnest.

It didn't take long for Brother Fountain to become bored with my newfound mental strength. So, when the bags tore as I was transferring the bucket to the kitchen, he refused to replace them. I continued on with the toilets and began singing hymns as my bare hands collected the foul pasty debris. This enraged him, and he told me to stop singing. I smiled demurely and said, "Yes sir." His face turned so red, I thought I'd have to clean up his exploded head as well.

I completed my task, making sure to keep the smile on my face, making a concerted effort to have him see it. When I finished, the room was spotless. My hands were ablaze with chemical irritation from the cleansers required to complete my task. He called out to my watcher telling her to return me to the dorm. I brazenly said, "Good night, sir" as I exited his space. I saw a renewed wave of fury as his fists clenched so tightly at his sides that they turned white. I had won, and we both knew it.

The next day infection began to show. My hands were an impossible shade of red, and swelling had begun. The micro cuts from scouring the pot the previous day had easily allowed the infiltration of the deification fluids into my body. For a time, I was still required to do the cleaning tasks which were assigned to the girls. By the end of the day, my fingers were spread as far apart as they could be from one another, yet still swelling into each other. Blisters which had begun to form, now accompanied the savage swelling. My hands were ablaze with pain.

Brother Fountain evaluated my hands, and surmised that I simply needed a regimen of saltwater baths to soak my hands in. This went on for 2 days despite the fact that I had infection lines running up my arms. My arms were so vividly marked, they looked as though they were a vein display for an anatomy class. I watched in fascination, as they spread, not knowing their presence meant my blood was infected, and I was in danger of dying.

When the lines reached my chest, they finally decided to take me to a doctor. I was under heavy watch, 3 people in total, to ensure I did not escape as we drove to Alabama in search of a doctor. I don't know that I saw a reputable doctor that day. I can't fathom a doctor seeing me in the condition I was presenting to them and not immediately admit me to a hospital, but I wasn't. I was given antibiotics, told to scrub my hands and arms to exfoliate the blisters and any scabs that formed, and soak them in iodine. I accepted the regimen, and we returned to the school. I was terrified I would die in that wretched place and never be found. I did as I was instructed, sobbing through the excruciating pain of breaking the blisters and subsequent scabs and soaking them in warm water and iodine accompanied by taking the medication. By some miracle I began to heal.

That series of events set the tone for my time at Bethel. Brother Fountain was constantly challenging me, but we both knew he had already dealt the worst he could, nearly killing me in the process. I survived countless licks with the thin, green swatches of brush that Brother Fountain or Brother Owens would choose. There were too many disciplinary running laps run around the huge open field which backed the properties buildings to bother counting, and along with the other girls, we were hired out by Brother Fountain to harvest farming fields in the nearby towns. We spent sometimes 15 hours a day, 6 days a week over the summer, working solidly to do the best we could in order to avoid his ruthless recourse, only to see Brother Fountain take the proceeds of our work and line his pockets. All this was done in the name of the Lord.

I was there for 13 months. The parental units never visited. They would call from time to time. My calls were always monitored, so I was never able to disclose how truly horrendous Bethel really was. I stayed in touch because even after everything Mother had done, I was not ready to break free. I couldn't yet acknowledge that there would never be the mother/daughter relationship I wanted, and still hoped for. I stayed in touch because I was terrified of what would happen to me in Bethel, afraid I would just die or disappear, and no one would find me. I was afraid Brother Fountain would kill me and lie about it and no one would know or care.

I was flown home for a visit with the parental units and my brother. It was supposed to be a two-week visit. Once I exited the plane, I saw them walking towards me. I ran and swooped up John, my tears running down both our faces. But at 4 years of age, I was an odd acquaintance of a sister to him, and that stung. I politely hugged my parental units, and we headed home.

I was not really acclimating back into home life. Knowing I was going back to Bethel in two weeks, I was subdued, and did not engage with anyone except John. Things were quiet at the house as we felt each other out. I spent my time seeing if I even wanted to fit back in, and the parental units struggled to get a read on me.

We had our simple routine. There was the small talk and niceties. We went to church. I'd go grocery shopping with the parental units, play with John, and spend time in my favorite swing, sliding into the cracked rubber, swaying in the easy June breeze, my red hair tickling my face as I spun through the air. We would eat dinner with the TV on, sitting in uneasy conversation, finishing with me falling into old patterns of clearing the table and doing the dishes before going to bed.

I had been home for less than a week when it happened. We had sat down to dinner when the TV announced that Bethel Baptist Academy had been taken over by the state. I ran into the living room, standing in front of the bulky TV as I watched the national news disclose people I knew being filed into busses, to be ushered off to a hospital, while Brother Owens, Brother Fountain and others in positions of authority were arrested for crimes committed against the kids at Bethel.

I was grateful I wasn't there when all that went down. I don't think I would have had the flight back home from my parental units that my visit granted me. I was almost 18 when all of that happened. I think Mother would have ridden out my remaining days until I turned 18 and left me for myself. Who knows, but I'm immensely glad I didn't have to find that out the hard way. I do know the look on Mother's face was not a happy one when I didn't return to Bethel.

GET OUT

I tried my best to fit back in. I did not want to let anybody down, so for a while, I walked a very dedicated line. I started feeling more comfortable being back home. The parental units even seemed cautiously comfortable. For a time, everything was fine. John and I grew closer, and our days together were tangled in love, adventure, and pranks. Being the older sister, I did have great fun with him, telling him such stories as a crusty hard piece of leather was a part of the sun, pulling his hand back, telling him he would be burnt to a crisp. He believed me for some time, and it became something we would joke about when he discovered the truth. We would also play games in the back of the car when we were out at night. My favorite game was seeing who could duck down and avoid being "burned" by the headlights, pretending that the cars were the enemy, seeking to destroy us. It was the skill we needed to survive in our world. Kittens pounce, puppies wrestle, and we darted out of sight.

Then there was the time when I fed him cat food. He initially looked at me in disbelief but when I popped a few kibbles in my mouth, he followed suit. He did not care for it, and I got a chuckle out of it. When Mother got wind of my prank, she did not appreciate the joke. I figured I wasn't having him do anything I hadn't done, and I tried to convey that to Mother, but it only frustrated her even more. Apparently, cat food was fine for me, but not for John.

I quickly discovered that the schooling I had completed at Bethel did not count towards my education in the public school system. Not only that, but had I graduated from Bethel there were only a few colleges that would have accepted my high school education and allowed me to apply. This frustrated me because my Bethel education meant nothing. My educational options were to go back to school as an 18-year-old sophomore or get my GED. I completed and passed my GED.

Upon turning 18, the parental units told me I had to get a job and pay something towards rent. The rent was not anything outrageous, and despite their parenting, this was one thing I understood the value in. It gave me a small sense of pride in taking care of myself and being responsible. I quickly became employed. I enjoyed my job and made friends. As a result, I was invited to go hang out with my new friends as they launched into their own adventures as new adults.

Having turned 18, I was of the opinion that the house rules would change. That seemed to be a natural progression for newly minted adults finding their way in the world. At least that was what I was observing among my other friends. I quickly discovered that was not the case in Mother's house. There was one occasion I told her I would be back late. She asked who I would be hanging out with, where I would be, what I would be doing, and what my idea of late was. I obliged her with the requested information, feeling that 11 pm on a Friday was reasonable. She refused my request, telling me I knew the house rules, and nothing had changed. Thus started my downward spiral. The realization that being 18 would have no impact on the rules was something that was hard for me to accept, and something Mother clarified as being non-negotiable.

Thankfully, Cynthia and I had reconnected, and I spent a vast amount of my time with her. Cynthia was still favored by Mother, so she again allowed me to spend the night at Cynthia's house without question, not realizing the reality of Cynthia's own home situation. We were both in rough places and found great solitude in each other. Her father had set up an RV in the back of the house as a get away from her stepmother, and we would spend countless hours soaking in each other's company, trying on different outfits, applying makeup, sampling different hairstyles, or sometimes singing to Wham!, Madonna, Michael Jackson, or Erasure as we danced around the tiniest of spaces. For me, there with her, it felt like a palace. Those are some of my most cherished memories of our friendship.

As Cynthia's abode became more like a home to me, Mother grew bitter of my time being spent with Cynthia. With time I started paying for it with guilt trips about not spending time with my own family. Mother had worked herself into a corner though in allowing me freer rein to hang out with Cynthia. When I called her out on that, Mother began to refuse my requests to hang out with Cynthia out of spite. With that, I began sneaking out again.

I planned on sneaking out to spend time with friends that lived in the mountains. I readied myself for bed, said goodnight, and settled into bed. I knew the parental units would check in on me. They did not disappoint. There was an entry by Mother into my bedroom to see if I was feeling okay. I chuckled internally, knowing she was feigning concern as an excuse to have come into my room. After stating I was just tired, Mother retreated back to the living room.

I faced away from the bedroom door, knowing another round was coming. When it happened, I feigned being asleep, careful to submerge my head onto the billowing comforter. I figured if they were to peek in again it would seem normal that my head was buried. Mother came over to the bed, and not seeing my face, reached out to confirm I was there. She stood there for a moment listening to my slow breathing. Satisfied, she left, closing the door behind her.

Still, I waited anxiously for them to go to bed. I listened to the night sounds, trying to block out the chirping crickets, and the sounds of the cool fall breeze as I listened for the telltale sounds of their settling in for the evening. Once everything was quiet, and sometime after their lights were turned off; I prepped my bed, and on the balls of my feet, quietly slipped out the door and into the night.

I missed the last bus of the evening. My friends lived a few miles away, so I started walking to their house. I figured I could catch the first bus the next morning if I couldn't get a ride home or didn't want to walk back. I was familiar with the mountain roads, as well as the sounds of the night air. I felt free as I found my way into the night, letting my eyes adjust to the heavy blue hues of night. I walked the empty roads to my friend's house and joined the party.

The night was relaxing. There was beer, weed and music. We all sat on the floor of the house, taking turns telling stories about ourselves, playing games, choosing music, and sharing hits of weed. I discovered a whole collection of Prince music I had never heard and was enthralled with his highly sexualized lyrics. Very late into the evening I made my exit and started the walk back home. I was lost in thought as the sultry lyrics infused into my brain. The walk seemed momentary, and before I realized it, I was back home.

Coming up to the house, nothing looked out of the place. All the lights were off, and everything was quiet. I came up to the door, expecting to hear the slightest squeak as the knob turned, but there was no turn. It was locked. I tried all the doors, only to find them all locked, even the car doors, which were never locked, forbade my entrance. All the windows were closed. In an act of desperation, I pulled off a screen, and pushed against the small kitchen window that doubled as ventilation during cooking. It gave way, and I slid the window open. I slowly shimmied my athletic frame through the small opening. Once through, I closed the window behind me, and went into my room. I knew I had fucked myself by sneaking out. Not knowing what would happen to me in the morning, I fell into what was most assuredly my last night of sleep in the house.

Morning came too quickly. I awoke to Father slamming the bedroom door behind him, both for effect and to wake me up. I startled into a groggy sitting position in bed and looked at him in silence. He asked me how the fuck I got in. In all my years I had never, ever heard Father cuss. I told him I got in through the kitchen window. Panicking, I asked why I couldn't be out later now that I was 18. I was desperate to justify why I had snuck out, so I challenged him regarding the rules. I told him I was following the same rules as when I was 13, and although I had spoken to Mother about it, things didn't seem reasonable now that I was 18. Although stating the obvious, it was the reason for my frustration. I thought perhaps he would concede and talk with Mother about setting up a new arrangement. He didn't respond, but spun around, slamming the door again behind him. I sat and waited, knowing Mother would be in shortly.

She came in with a vengeance, throwing two suitcases at me as I sat in the bed. Her only words to me were "get out," yelled at the top of her lungs. Having snuck out, I realized this was the new arrangement. I packed as much as I could, said goodbye to John and my cat, Koshka. I was terrified to leave, but also had an odd, newfound feeling of freedom. I had been seeking escape but hadn't gathered enough money together to branch out on my own. I headed out down the road. Without any place to go, Cynthia let me stay with her even though her situation was not any better. We rallied together to find a better existence for both of us.

CHICKEN POX

It's a wonderful thing finding a way in the world, but it's also delicate, and prone to fractures. I had hammered, carved, and refined my place in the existence of this world. It was rarely pretty, but it was mine, and I held it close to my heart, owning it all. I did the best I could, which included doing my best to be kind and helpful.

I had become part of yet another church, this one being of my own choosing. I immersed myself in the college group, which met twice a week. I enjoyed so many of the people there and felt good in my heart for going. Part of finding peace for me was in being a good friend to others. That, in turn made me feel good about myself. So, when one of my fellow adult youths and his grandmother needed a ride to the airport, I didn't think twice before offering. We agreed on a pickup location for them and called it good.

The morning of the needed ride, I woke up not feeling at all well. I felt woozy, lightheaded, had a temperature, and red spots on my tummy. I called and asked if there was any way they could find another ride but was promptly told no. I could tell he was irritated at my asking, but I explained my symptoms and he still agreed to the ride, stating it was too late for him to attempt to get one from someone else. I said that was fine, figuring I would take them, come back home and rest. I picked them up and we were off, traveling over highway 17 to the San Jose airport.

I dropped them both off, giving my friend a brief hug before we parted ways. I hopped into my old grey VW Rabbit and headed back home in the heavy rain, feeling disoriented, hot, and very weak. The red spots on my tummy had turned into angry blisters. Having no idea what they were, I was panicking. I was on my way, headed home toward highway 17 from 880 South when my car failed me. I was cruising along, when suddenly, my car started sputtering, jolting erratically on the highway. I was able to make it over to the shoulder of the road before coming to a stop, my dead car doing nothing more than keeping me dry.

I sat there for some time, shivering in the cold, yet feeling too weak to make the walk to the exit. I gave up hope for help when I saw a CHP vehicle drive by without stopping. I knew I needed to make the walk as this was before cell phones were an everyday part of life. I bundled up as best I could, grabbed change for a pay phone, and ventured out along the highway. Thinking I would just be driving, I was ill prepared, having no jacket, umbrella, or any warm clothes. I was exhausted by the time I reached the exit, and when I reached a pay phone at the gas station, I collapsed into the box, too weak to make a call.

I eventually slid myself up the glass enclosure. I wearily pulled the phone off the receiver, pushed the change into the slot, and slowly dialed Mother's number, breathing heavily into the phone waiting for her to pick up. I almost gave up when I heard her on the line. I told her my situation, making sure to explain how sick I felt. I knew if it was just about the car, she wouldn't help me. I described my fever, and included the weird blisters on my tummy, that had expanded to other parts of my body. I also told her how incredibly hot I felt. I told her I had been hot when I left, so despite the rain, I did not dress for the weather. I said I needed help to get home and asked her to come get me. I knew better than to ask for help with the car.

The phone was silent for a minute. I could hear her leveled breathing. After a moment she started with "well," before saying that she couldn't pick me up. I started crying on the phone, desperate for help, only to be told that she didn't want John to contract chicken pox, which is what she thought I had. She told me she wished me luck and hung up.

I shoved more money into the phone and called a friend who was at work. I told him about my car, feeling ill and Mother thinking I had chicken pox, and refusing to help me. He asked where he could call me back and told me to wait there. I did, and he called back shortly to let me know he was on his way. He not only helped me get home, but he helped me get my car back as well.

I did have chicken pox as a young adult, and it was a brutal recovery. The scares riddled my back with a few on my face as well, but I made a full recovery. I came to discover that John had in fact already had the chicken pox when Mother had told me she didn't want him to catch them. She amended what she said to say he had a very light case of the pox and didn't want him to catch them again. I looked at her as she unveiled this latest lie, letting it roll off her tongue like water off a duck's back. Even then I knew how a virus worked and the likelihood of him contracting chicken pox again was slight. I never understood why Mother made efforts to appear caring when it was just so obvious that she wasn't. Like so many other things, I let it slide to the back of my memory, where so many of my interactions with her lived.

A HYPOTHESIS

In spite of the darkness of our relationship, there were moments of light with Mother. It was those light interactions that kept me going throughout all the years, thinking I would finally reach a point where I was worthy of Mother's love. I had a good stretch with her in my twenties and thirties. Although it would be off and on. I would go to the house for lunch or dinner. We would all laugh, eat, and engage as a family. Those are moments I cherished. I felt that I had finally made some strides in our relationship.

We would often go for walks in the mountain area I had grown up in. As we weaved our way through the redwoods, we would talk about a lot of different things. It was probably the closest to friendly we had ever been. It was on these walks I felt that maybe, just maybe there would be healing. All those hopes came to a standstill on one such walk when I caught her in another lie.

We were striding along the road in easy conversation, talking about her and Father. The afternoon air was cool on our faces as Mother spoke of how they met. She regaled me with her desire to meet Father when they were in high school. She had asked a friend to introduce them, but her friend would not, telling Mother they would not be a good match. Stubborn as ever, Mother took matters into her own hands, and introduced herself to Father. Mother said things went well, and they started dating in high school, and were later married.

She ended with gushing over the number of years they had been married. I thought they had been married longer. I corrected her because the number of years she boasted being married meant they had gotten married while she was pregnant with me. She stammered out the correction, but I could tell I had just caught her in a lie. I called her on it, and her face went from red with embarrassment to pale with panic. It was a moment she couldn't come up with another lie fast enough, so she admitted they were married while she was pregnant with me. She went on to say they didn't want me to ever feel that they had married because of me, so they had added a year of marriage.

I thought it was ridiculous, at least her excuse was. At the time, I whole-heartedly thought they didn't want me to know they were having sex outside marriage, so they lied to me. Later that day, Mother told Father of our conversation. He avoided me for the rest of my visit. For a while, each time I visited, he would either avoid me or not look me in the eye. I wondered if he was embarrassed that I knew he had sex before they were married. It made sense seeing that they had spent my entire life berating me about saving myself for marriage. It didn't make sense why he would distance himself from me. We were all adults at this point. With time his self-imposed isolation faded, and so I let it go.

As I grew older, the internet and web searches became more and more accessible for information. Knowing my birth was during a pivotal time in the Vietnam War, I had always wondered how Father had evaded the war. Mother had told me he had a low draft number, and that was why he was never called to serve. I had always taken her at her word, but as I grew older, I became more curious, and suspicious. Filled with desire for truth, I began to do research.

Father's draft number was 10, so Mother was right, Father did have a low draft number. However, my research rendered that draft numbers were called randomly, and his draft number had in fact been called in 1970. Mother never told me that Father would have been required to report for duty on October 31, 1970.

I understood there were different classifications for individuals who were required to report for duty. I began looking into the parameters within each of those and discovered if someone had a child who was reliant on them for basic life necessities, those individuals could be relieved from duty under draft classification 3-A. That classification lists a hardship to their dependents. Although it was still being pieced together, the puzzle as to why Father seemed so ashamed was slowly becoming clearer.

The draft was reinstated December 1, 1969. My hypothesis is that Father and Mother knew his draft number and knew he would have to report the following year. His escape for serving relied on two conditions. Marrying Mother and having a child before his date to appear for duty. They would have had to act fast, and they did. They closed out 1969 together, with Mother being newly pregnant with me. They married early in 1970. I was born in September, and Father never went to war.

If I am correct, Mother lied about literally everything surrounding the beginning of their lives together... when they married, why they married, why I was conceived. I believe I was conceived to rescue Father from war, and they were married to legitimize his need to stay stateside, away from Vietnam. I was a strategic pawn played in a game, hopeless to its end. The only assured outcome was Father did not go to war. It's no wonder why Mother despised me. Father was the only one who really benefited from the arrangement. As far as Mother was concerned, I was just a constant reminder of everything she had given up. All of her anger, frustration, and resentment in her choices bled into every corner of my relationship with her.

COLLEGE

Being a young adult, living on my own in a very expensive county was challenging to say the least. There were times where I lived off Taco Bell, canned soup, beans, and rice. There was no real need for a refrigerator because I had no excess of food. Housing was always a challenge. I rented rooms with strangers, and later with friends. There were a few months where I was homeless, living out of my car, relying on friends for couch surfing.

It wasn't until I was in my mid to late 20's that I had finally "arrived," making barely enough money to live on my own. I was thrilled to have my own space, and happily sacrificed healthy eating to supplement my newly found feeling of success. Going home took on new meaning, and I would often sit in my living room relishing in the fact that the space was all mine.

Before conquering that milestone, I had reached a realization. I missed school. I began regretting my decision to cut school in retaliation towards the parental units. I realized that ultimately, I was the only one who really suffered from my decision. Sure, it angered the parental units, and in the moment, I felt I had distributed the only retaliation I could towards them. It had been a way of channeling my anger and frustration, but at its core served no purpose for me, and actually ended up handicapping me. I was smarter than that, and really should have just been successful despite my circumstances. Anger and rage had blinded me, and in those precious moments I let it happen. I reached a point where I saw my worth and the worth of education in my life. I wanted to better myself, both mentally as well as financially. With that, the desire to go to college blossomed.

I had no idea how to pursue college. I really wish I had sought out an academic counselor for advice. I was unaware that financial aid was a possibility for me. Because of finances, and the fact I had not attended school in a few years, I decided to start small. I fumbled around as best I could, registering myself in the college system. I took a volleyball class with a friend, which I really enjoyed. I ended up taking the class several times. I looked at other classes, but quickly realized that between tuition, books, and other school fees, I did not make enough money to go to school full time.

I struggled with ideas for financing, which included taking on multiple jobs. I was concerned that after so many years of not really studying, I would not have the time I needed to study if I took on more work. I had tried taking a single academic class, but even that was challenging, and with no real study habits, I withdrew from the class out of fear of failing. I talked to a work friend, who said her parents were helping her pay for her education and not knowing my situation, suggested I ask my own.

I pondered what my friend had said. It was during a period of time when things were better between Mother and I. She had often made comments about wishing she had pursued her completion of college, so I thought maybe, just maybe, she would help. I outlined my discussion with her, researching the basic costs of school and books. I thought I could switch to part time work while I was in school to help supplement rental costs. I rehearsed conversations surrounding my request being specifically for a loan, and I would pay them back when I began a career. I even decided I wanted to go into nursing or dental hygiene. The prerequisites were similar, so I had time to decide while I was in school. I practiced this conversation for weeks, growing excited over the possibility of becoming a successful college student, imagining the doors a college degree would open for me.

During the weeks leading up to my asking, Mother and I continued to do well. I would discuss the idea of going to college without having a financial discussion. She was receptive to the idea, even telling me she thought I would benefit from it. As these conversations continued, I became more hopeful she would be willing to help me financially.

I had decided the day had arrived. I began the conversation discussing my desires for financial freedom and scholastic success. My prepping paid off, and my delivery was flawless. I started to embark on the discussion of a loan to aid in my success. I did not get through but about two sentences before I was cut off with a scoff escaping Mother's lips.

She flatly told me no. She went on to say that they had already invested any college money they would have supplied me with, into my stay at Bethel. She said there was no desire to supply me any more money, even as a loan. I mentioned that she didn't "supply" me the money, and it was her choice to send me to Bethel, not mine. I was then told I had left her no choice by my actions. She suggested I make sure I marry a man who could take care of me financially. She said that way I would either not have to work, or he could fund my education. With that, the conversation was done, as was the rapport we had built up to that moment.

It was years before I returned to college, and it was never full time. I took one or two classes at a time, doing the best I could with what I was given. Thankfully, I finished strong. In the end, I had the support I needed to finally get my degree, and made the Dean's list while doing it, without ever having any help or support from Mother. I was incredibly proud of that. So much so that I never told her I had accomplished a college degree. My silence didn't matter. I completed it for myself, not for her. It felt good to owe her absolutely nothing, including the information that I had achieved my goal.

CELEBRATION

As a young adult, one of the many things I did was to visit my grandmother. I had not seen her in many years. Although I missed her terribly, without transportation I had no way to drive the several hours necessary to see her. That being said, I was extremely excited when my boyfriend, Brian, and I decided to visit her. I felt so rebellious doing something I knew Mother would not approve of. More than that was the elation of being able to see her and spend a few cherished moments with her.

The three of us sat around making small talk, trying to catch up. Brian, knowing I hadn't seen her in years, mostly just watched an old relationship rekindle in the warm summer afternoon. We parted ways with words of encouragement to stay in contact. I do wish I had done a better job at that, but I did not.

We traveled back home, enjoying the drive. I was so thankful he made the drive with me. I was glad that he had the chance to meet her. He was one of only a few of my friends that did. They both seemed impressed with each other. Brian was my first serious relationship, and of all the people in my life, my grandmother's approval was more important to me than anyone else's.

Things progressed on, and I got caught up in surviving life as an adult. I didn't make good on my plans to stay in touch with Grandma. Before I knew it, she was getting ready to celebrate a milestone birthday. There was going to be a big fan fair, and the whole family was supposed to be there. Mother told me about the event shortly before its date. I had already made plans with Brian to attend another event, so I told her I wouldn't be going. Keep in mind all the birthdays I endured with Mother growing up, another birthday seemed more painful then celebratory, and I failed to see the importance of it.

Mother kept hounding me to go. She said it was more important than any event I had planned. I questioned her how it could possibly be more important when she had just spent numerous years forbidding me to see Grandma. She was irritated by that, and switched to manipulative tactics, telling me if I loved my grandmother, I would go. I told her that wasn't fair, and my going had no reflection as to my love for her, I told Mother I simply had other plans that were also important. We went rounds about the party. Being young, stubborn, and officially out of Mother's immediate control, I told her I was not going. Ultimately, I didn't go just so I could tell Mother no and watch as she could really do nothing about it. I was young and immature, and was high off her inability to force me, as well as her frustration over that fact.

Once again, I chose the moment of victory over the true celebration. Grandmother's birthday ended up being a wonderful party for a lovely woman. Included in the festivities was a family portrait. Three generations of family all present, except me. It was the last generational family portrait that was taken. I regret letting my hatred of

Mother's grappling for control ruin a special moment with someone I truly loved.

Hope Doran

DOES IT REALLY MATTER?

I had settled into a rented room in Capitola. At the time I thought it was a safe choice. The room was part of a very small apartment owned by a woman in a wheelchair. She was a retired model, and when we met, I was both struck by the fact she was in a wheelchair and the stark variance of her jet-black hair against the palest skin I had ever seen. Her eyebrows looked as though they were painted onto her face and sat in high arcs above her almost black eyes. When she spoke, it was in a whispery voice, and I had to strain to hear her. She was odd but seemed fine.

It wasn't my first choice for a living arrangement, but the price was very affordable. I moved my modest belongings in and went on about my daily life. I was always busy between work and friends, and she became irritated with me. I didn't know it at the time, but she thought she would have a companion moving in, someone to keep her company, eat with her and help her cook. I had no interest in any of those things. The one time I did sit down to a meal with her, she would not stop talking, telling me one story after another of her life before the accident that landed her in the wheelchair. I fidgeted with the decorative candleholder as she hammered on about her life, lost in thought over how I could exit the situation and go to bed.

She finally stopped to take a sip of wine. I jumped up, and began clearing the table, telling her I was tired. I did the dishes under her watchful eye. She made me feel incredibly uncomfortable as she scrutinized my work. Once I finished, I went to bed, only to be woken up by her eerie, whispery voice beckoning me. I tried ignoring it, pretending as if I was already asleep, but she started banging on the bedroom door.

Fearing she would open it; I opened my bedroom door. She ushered me back towards the dining room table. She wheeled over to the table, facing it, asking me to look at the candleholders, "whisper yelling" at me to fix it. I did not immediately see what was wrong, so I made the mistake of asking her. It turned out in my fidgeting I had not lined the two candleholders back up. She was yelling at me to fix it, telling me how stupid I was for not noticing and correcting it on my own. I walked over, shoved the holder the two inches it needed, bringing it back to alignment, looked at her and said, "really?" She started hissing at me as I retreated to my room. Not talking in whispery tones, legitimately hissing at me as if she were a snake.

Once I was back to my room, I realized how frightened of the woman I was. I had my suitcase in the closet, so I pulled it out and used it to block the door, knowing full well she would not be able to get in. There was just enough room for me to slide in and out the door. I sat on my bed and cried, pondering my life. It was the first time as an adult I questioned where I was in life, and how I wanted to live. I had slipped away from the church I attended, thinking it no longer served me, but began to feel that maybe I should return to it.

I kept the suitcase in front of the door so the woman would not be able to have access to me or rummage through my things. It ended up being a good call, because the woman complained about not being able to get into my room. I told her it was my space, not hers. She didn't like this, and one night, when I was at a church function, she had her son come and move the suitcase so she could have access. She went through my things, making no effort to hide the fact she was invading my privacy. In the beginning she was seemingly harmless, but she ended up being someone who I could not wait to escape from.

Having reconnected with church, it opened doors to rekindle friendships, and I was able to move out in short order. I told the woman why I was moving out, but I don't think she cared. It felt good to be free of her, and as I attended church regularly, I began to heal from my experience with her. Once immersed, I recalled why I enjoyed church so much. It offered solitude in my tumultuous life. The commodity of other young adults trying to find their way in the world was healing and resonated with me as well. My friendships there, which included Cynthia, saved my life.

Mother and I were talking off and on about church. It was weird, but I think she resented the fact that I was so thoroughly enjoying my church, but more so, that I was finding peace within it. Just like so many other things in my life, she set out to manipulate me, working on passive aggressive conversation regarding going to her church.

It started out simple enough. She would simply ask me to attend her church. I preferred the Saturday night services at my own church, so I could attend the college group Sunday morning and still have some of the morning to myself. I told her that, and she grew more persistent, shifting to telling me that as an unmarried woman, I was required to fall under my Father's rule, which included attending church with them.

Irritated, I started going with them on Sunday. I did not care for the stuffy evangelical church setting. I did not benefit from it in any way. In my seemingly unending desire to please Mother, I went for a fair amount of time. Mother was stiff with me because I was not presenting as the doting daughter, she wanted me to appear as. It became yet another thorn of contention between us.

Having had my first experience with my previous housing situation, I boldly attempted to have a more direct conversation with her. I told her I didn't feel like her church was a good fit for me, and I would be returning to my own. She looked at me, and point blank told me that in doing that I was falling out of favor with God. She stated again that I was to be under my Father's rule until I was married. I told her I didn't think that would be an issue with God seeing they had kicked me out of the house. I continued, saying I believed it was more important to attend a church that I found myself growing in rather than attend one simply for the sake of attending it. She looked at me, smirked, and told me to believe what I wanted, I would find out how wrong I was at Christ's return. I'm still waiting for the return of Christ, but also still confident in my decision.

BRIAN

Brian was a light in my life. He was charming, handsome, caring, and charismatic. When he told me he liked me, I about fell down out of shock. We grew close quickly, and soon became inseparable. We were both trying to figure things out in life. He was a college student, and I, a new dental assistant.

After we returned from visiting my grandmother we carried on, falling more in love. Perhaps foolishly in love at such a young age, but there you have it. We would talk about our future, where we wanted to live and the things we would do. After months of courting, Brian gave me a promise ring. I was over the moon.

We wanted to do everything right. We prayed a lot about marriage, talked about planning for a possible wedding, and what that looked like. Together we decided to move forward with conversation of marriage with a counselor at our church. We met with him weekly for months, seeking his guidance and counsel in moving forward. The biggest thing we were dealing with was the fact that Brian wanted my parents' permission to marry me. He would absolutely not marry me without it.

So, once again I was at the mercy of Mother to do something in my favor. My heart sank, but I loved Brian and was willing to do everything in my power to garner favor and have them say yes to his request for acceptance. Mother had made zero attempts to meet or spend time with him, and Father followed suit for a long time. At my request, father and I would eventually meet weekly to talk about my relationship with Brian. I truly felt that Brian and I were a beautiful fit for partnership, and I did my best to convey that to Father.

Things were stagnant for months. I was in a stalemate. Brian and I would meet with the marriage counselor to discuss this impasse. Brian got to the point he was comfortable with having only Father's permission. He saw that as something plausible, but I knew better. It seemed Father rarely did anything without Mother's approval, so I did not see the situation as any different, and I sadly began to see the end of our relationship.

I asked Father to meet with both Brian and myself, and he agreed. We met at the small apartment I lived in. We all anxiously sat around the table, drinking coffee, and discussing the possibility of acceptance of a wedding. Father evaded the question, not saying yes or no. At the point we parted ways, neither Brian nor I thought it would render the result we wanted.

We returned to our pastor, asking advice. The pastor suggested a meeting with the parental units, and us to see if we could get an answer as to why they would not accept a marriage union. That seemed like a good idea, so I suggested it to Mother, knowing full well any yes or no answer from either of them would originate with her. She agreed, but only if she could bring her pastor with them to the meeting. I agreed, and the meeting was set.

We met at our church the next afternoon. Our pastor was doing his best to set everyone at ease, but I could tell from the start Mother was ready to leave before she arrived. She went through the introductions, saving a curt, icy hello for Brian before sitting down and folding her arms across her chest. Brian did his best to make things as concise as he could. He could sense he was on borrowed time. He finished and the room was silent for a moment before our pastor went to speak up. Mother did not let him finish. She looked at Brian, and said, "Listen, I don't doubt your love for Jesus, or my daughter, but you are not the one for her. I will never, ever give my blessing for your marriage to her. Do you understand me?"

The room froze as we all took in what just happened. We heard Mother's chair creak as she leaned back to grab her purse. She stood, looked at Father and their pastor and said, "We're done here," before exiting the office. Father and their pastor gathered themselves and shuffled out after her. I watched them exit, the door slowly coming back to rest as it closed. Not only was the door closing to the room, but on all hope of marriage to Brian. Despite the love we had, it was not enough for Brian to move forward without the parental units' blessing.

He broke up with me shortly after. I made requests to seek out acceptance through other avenues in the church. It wasn't the church he wanted acceptance from; it was from a woman who never even accepted me. He was asking the impossible in wanting the blessing for marriage from someone who had crushed so many of my dreams simply because they were mine, and not hers. I don't feel that she truly cared about me, my desires, or what I thought was best for my own life.

The next person I dated, Mother gushed over incessantly. She never missed a moment to tell me how godly he was or how much she thought we made a good fit. She told me he was my soul mate. Still wanting her acceptance, I bought into what she was feeding me. We ended up getting married.

Brian, ever true to me, pulled me aside and suggested my upcoming marriage was too hasty. I said, "Well, at least I have Mother's blessing." I could tell my words stung him, but he was right, I never should have married the man. We were not compatible in any way to cohabitate as a married couple. I broke his heart trying to gain some sort of acceptance from Mother. I was seeking an acceptance that never came. It was grossly unfair to him, and I regret I wasn't a stronger human to have just said no.

At one point shortly after I had been married, I had asked for her help in working things out with my then husband. Mother told me that she had no place in that discussion, and I needed to figure it out on my own. Despite my desperate pleas for guidance in being successful as a wife, I was coldly told I should pray about it and figure it out on my own. The rejection from a woman who should have been a support, a resource, a confidant was a bitter pill to swallow. Instead of offering help or encouragement, she shunned me. I was left once again feeling that no matter what I did, I would never be enough. Not wanting to have a discussion regarding the failure of my marriage, I chose to shut her out.

Hope Doran

GRADUATION

It was a day to celebrate! My brother was graduating from junior high school. I had to research the information because I had not spoken with the parental units in several years. In spite of that, my brother was important to me, and I wanted to be there and celebrate his accomplishment. Even if it meant I was going to be unnoticed.

It was a long road getting to the point where I decided to attend his graduation ceremony. I had become so resentful of Mother, and everything that had happened regarding a hasty marriage, and even hastier breakup. The 5 years had passed quickly, and I had yet to speak with either parental unit. Now in my mid-20s, I still missed my time with my brother, but I was not at a point where I could engage Mother following the end of my marriage.

I debated for weeks over going to the graduation, and whether or not I would take the opportunity to rekindle conversation with the parental units. I had a very dear friend who was supportive of me. He told me I should do what I felt was right for my brother as well as myself. He and I had discussed at great length my dilemma, and I decided to just be present and be a silent support for my brother.

The day of the graduation, I was so nervous. I finally decided what to wear, grabbed the card I was certain I would not give my brother, and drove to the Civic Center where the graduation was to take place. I exited my car, and walked into the facility, completely on edge. I was looking for my brother as well as looking for the parental units. I decided to sit high in the seats so that I could survey the crowd and find them, undetected.

It didn't take long. I watched as the parental units came in and took a seat close to the floor level. They were beaming, smiling ear to ear, as they conversed with each other. I could tell they were proud of their son, and I recalled never seeing that look on their faces regarding me. It made me sad and jealous, but that was not my brother's doing, and I reminded myself of that as a quick flicker of resentment burrowed into my heart.

The ceremony went wonderfully. I hooted and hollered for my brother, willing him to know I was there. I watched mother whip her head around, as I hollered. I don't know if John knew I was there, but Mother surely did. I could see it on her face. It was the look of being startled, seeking out to find the culprit of her fear, uneasy in her lack of success. Her newfound knowledge showed her I was willing and able to be a part of my brother's life without her permission.

I followed them around after the ceremony, wanting desperately to stride up to them, confident in who I was, failures and all. I wanted to hug my brother as I told him I missed him, and that I was proud of him. I wanted to look Mother in the eye and challenge her to dismiss me. I watched as they doted on John, and watched John react happily in his moment. I realized if I went up to them that would be what my brother would remember of the day. I didn't trust Mother to not make a scene, casting me away in front of my brother and anyone around who wanted to watch. Not wanting to ruin his celebration, I retreated into the crowd, disappearing onto the cement sidewalk, and back to my waiting friend.

He told me he was proud of me. I told him I wasn't because I didn't let John know I was there. He said it didn't matter, there would come a day when I would be able to tell him. He gave me a much-needed hug and I cried in his arms.

Hope Doran

LOSS

I was at work when I got the call. Grandma was dying. I was told that they had contacted Mother several times in an attempt to get a hold of me because Grandma wanted to see me. Mother repeatedly told them that she didn't know where I was. All of that changed when Grandma became terminal. Suddenly Mother knew where I was, and even provided them with a phone number to reach me.

It was an odd combination of feelings as I drove to see Grandma. Through the tears of an inevitable loss, I was furious at Mother for withholding my information when it was requested. Mother was always good at causing divides, but for some reason it still came as a hostile surprise to me. Renewed anger evaporated my long drive, and before I knew it, I had arrived.

I pulled up, jumped out of my Jeep, and ran to the front door of my aunt's home. We had not seen each other in years, and hugged briefly before she ushered me into Grandma's room. We locked eyes as I scurried to her and embraced her frail body in a hug. I heard her say over my shoulder, now I have what I wanted. That broke me. I started sobbing, regretting, and apologizing for not spending more time with her. She said she understood. She said she loved me and was so glad I was there. I took her graceful, manicured hand in mine, and stroked her pale pink polished fingers as she caught me up on things she had done, adventures she had had, and the more painful discussion of her cancer, and the limited time we had to share.

I was there every waking moment I could be. Sometimes I would go after work, making the long drive in rush hour traffic to see her just one more time. All of my weekends were hers. We would sit and chat. She took every opportunity to head to the kitchen and sit at the adjoining dining room table. It's like she knew there would come a time when she wouldn't be able to make the short walk down the hall, and she relished that space. One of us would assist her, walking in her vibrant red silk pajamas, talking lightheartedly as if time was not an enemy to making memories. It reminded me of the few times we were at her house when I was younger; we were always at the dining room table. That's where the magic happened for Grandma. My aunt strove to immerse Grandma in the experience, always making sure there was the smell of something delicious cooking, or the rich smell of coffee brewing to give Grandma the feel goods we all knew she wanted.

Before any of us were ready, the day came when she was confined to her bed. We would take turns spending time with her in the long days. When she was awake, she was still vibrant, thus bored, so we began to seek out ways to keep her entertained. For me, I would replace her grown out pink polish, rubbing her hands when the polish was dry. We would exchange the life stories we had missed out on. I would keenly watch her as she regaled me with tales from her past, rubbing her thumb against the fresh polish of her pinkie nail like it was a magic ball bringing forth the memory for her to tell.

Grandma had loved to paint and missed it. She was becoming more and more weak with every passing day, so the idea of a large-scale watercolor that she had so beautifully mastered was out of the question. I went to a pottery-painting place in my hometown called Petroglyph. I explained my grandmother's love for painting and needing to do something on a smaller scale. I told them she was bedridden and offered to buy the paints and other necessary supplies that are usually for in house use only. They kindly told me to take what I wanted with no limits and bring everything back with the final product for firing. Their kindness made me cry as I chose the colors, and brushes for the project. I decided plates would be the easiest to paint, so I chose that for the project.

At first Grandma was hesitant. This was not her usual media, but she was soon enjoying herself. She spoke of other projects she had painted, awards she had won, joking she wouldn't win any awards with the plate she was painting. We laughed, and I told her it would be my prize, and I would cherish it. She liked that and asked me to paint in some of the area around what she had painted, and watched in tired silence as I filled in the space around the red flower she had chosen to paint. I cried as I realized I had the last thing her talented hands would ever create.

She slipped into a permanent sleep shortly after that. We continued our time with her, taking turns talking to her, as she would tell us from behind closed eyes the people she was seeing who had passed decades before, like her parents, cousin, and brother. We sat as she mumbled conversations with them, smiling and occasionally even laughing, obviously at peace in her long-lost loved one's company. She went from one to another while she rested easy in the bed, even calling out family pets, such as Maggie, a dog they had. Long gone, save the memories. I would sit and listen to family members gather around her bed and tell stories of the people Grandma called out. I think we all felt a deep sense of peace knowing she was reconnecting with all those lost in her life that she still obviously cherished.

She died in her sleep. I regretted sleeping through her passing. My aunt told me when I woke up. We held each other and cried. I felt so much loss it was hard to function. She was truly a remarkable, amazing, and strongly loved woman. She deeply impacted my life on so many levels. I was so proud that she was mine, and even more proud that I was hers.

Memorial and funeral plans were made. Everyone who could be there was, save one… Mother. She never came to have healing words with Grandma while she was alive. Weeks earlier, when I was contacted about Grandma, it had been about 5 years since I had spoken with the parental units. When Father came, it was awkward, but manageable. I spoke with Mother briefly while Grandma was still alive. In spite of her coldness, I asked why she wouldn't come. She told me Grandma hated her, and the nicest thing she could do for Grandma was to not show up while she's on her deathbed. It amazed me that even after everything I encountered in my own experiences with Mother, I was still shocked by her heated answer.

Mother didn't leave it at that though. She didn't come to the memorial service, or the funeral. Not even to support her high school sweetheart of a husband as he grieved the loss of his mother, or any of the other family that was heavy laden with grief. When plans were made to fly back to Pennsylvania and lay Grandma to rest with Grandpa, I joined. There was no way I wouldn't be there for Grandma, my family, or myself. I saw a new level of low from Mother. She was completely void of a common factor within the quality of love... empathy. I knew she hated Grandma, but when she died, Mother remained cold. I can't speak for anyone else, but her icy refrain affected me. It was then I saw firsthand that she was capable and willing to treat everyone around her with the cold-hearted callousness I had only seen displayed towards me. I resented her for not being there. I resented her even more for not being there for Father. It spoke volumes of how little she really believed in family, in love, in support, in common decency for another human being beside herself.

Hope Doran

PREGNANCY

We had only been living together a short time when I found out I was pregnant. I was 28 years old and terrified. My then boyfriend was charming, but this was just so completely unexpected, and the product of using responsible, preventable measures to protect me from pregnancy. I kept my information to myself while I contemplated if I was even suitable to be a mother, and if I were, would I be prepared to be a single mother if my boyfriend did not want to take on that family role.

There really wasn't a whole lot of time needed. The life growing inside me was one I already loved. I decided I did not need to repeat the example my mother was. I could create my own experience, using what she had done to me as an example of what I did not want to do, and who I did not want to be. It wasn't a perfect plan, but it offered improvement over what I had to draw on as an example. As far as being a single parent, well, I had decided I was going to be okay with that as well if I needed to be.

Armed with my decision, I spoke with my boyfriend. He was ecstatic! We began making plans for our future as we daydreamed about being new parents. We began to formulate plans to transform a bedroom into a nursery as the days passed by quickly. My growing belly held our child that was dearly and powerfully loved before he had even taken his first breath.

My tummy grew quickly. It was amazing watching my form transition, making way for the baby growing inside me. My boyfriend would rub lotion on my growing belly every night, and talk to my tummy as I lay there, listening to all the things a new father would disclose to his unborn child. It was magical. During my days, I would sing to my baby as I drove here or there, rubbing my tummy as I went along. Between songs I would talk to my unborn child, expressing my love for him, telling him I would do my very best by him. I apologized for things not even done yet, but knowing I would not be perfect. It broke my heart to know that, but I told him I was reinventing the wheel as far as being a mother. I hoped someday he would understand and know despite everything, he was always cherished.

In our evenings, we would sit and relax on the couch. It seemed one of us always had our hands on my belly. Even our cats knew something was changing. They would sniff at my belly any time I was still, and one of the cats that had previously not been a lap cat would sit on me, laying her body across my belly purring incessantly as she kneaded my tummy.

I had delayed telling Mother. I knew she would not approve of any of it really. I hadn't even told her I lived with anyone yet. I decided to drop the bomb when I traveled up for dinner and to spend some time with my brother. Let me just say, I know how to silence a room when it comes to the parental units. I think John was the only one who was excited.

As time went on, I quickly outgrew any of my clothes. Mother offered to get me some maternity clothes. I should have known better. I should have said no. We went to a maternity store, where she proceeded to barrage me with how disgusting it was to see pregnant women showing their tummies. She went on to say women should cloak themselves when they are pregnant so they would not be noticed for their pregnancies. This went on for hours. By the time we left the store I was broken and embarrassed to be pregnant. Mother had me convinced I was showing yet another example of how utterly ungodly I really was.

She had bought me the most bland, muted clothes that were available. I proceeded through the rest of my pregnancy cloaked in drab colors immersed onto folds of frumpy fabric, having bought into Mother's teachings. It wasn't just my body I was hiding; it was my newfound embarrassment over being pregnant. She had single-handedly stolen my joy of being pregnant.

My boyfriend and I continued on through our days, preparing for our upcoming bundle of joy. We had found out we were going to have a boy and commenced with deciding on a name. We each wrote out 10 names we wanted. We then switched lists, and the other could cross off 5 of the names we didn't like, no questions asked. With the remaining 10 possibilities, we began research to see what the names meant.

During this time, John, who was my favorite (and only) pesky, then teenaged brother started begging us to name the baby after him. He was so persistent it became comical.

When we had narrowed it down to just a few possibilities, we came across the origins of the name Ian. It is the Scottish version of the name John. So, my brother got his wish. Within its origins, Ian was named after his Uncle John.

When it was coming down to the wire, I was beautifully gifted with multiple baby showers, which provided us an ample start into parenthood. We felt as ready as two expectant parents could be, embarking into parenthood with no experience. We were very excited to welcome Ian into our lives officially.

I was still two weeks from Ian's due date. Mother was relentless, telling me I was a big baby, weighing 9 pounds. She was convinced Ian would be as well. She kept going on and on about how all the baby clothes we had received would not fit him. She said he was for sure going straight to 3-month baby clothes (like she was a modern-day Nostradamus). She asked how many 3-month outfits we had, which was limited. She insisted on taking me to the store to select baby outfits in larger sizes so we would not be shorthanded. We figured Ian would end up in them eventually, and thought it was a nice gesture for Mother, so Mother and I went shopping.

Mother was a little excessive with the purchases. When we were done, the bill was over $300. I thanked her profusely; thinking this was such an incredibly kind, grandmotherly thing to do. I thought perhaps there was hope for the relationship between my mother and her first grandchild.

When we got back to the house, Mother made a big production of things. She had my boyfriend come out, and I showed him all the outfits. We both oohed and awed over everything, sensing Mother was looking for a big show of gratitude. When everything had been viewed, Mother looked at my boyfriend, handed him the receipts, and flatly told him he could pay her back with a check if he didn't have the cash on hand. He and I looked at each other, shocked. We had not planned for the expense, but he went and wrote out a check and handed it to Mother. She left shortly after, leaving us to process what just happened. We were upset over the fact she hadn't spoken to us about whether or not we could even afford such a purchase. It was such a hostile thing to do; we decided she was attempting to cause a rift between us, which almost happened. In the end my boyfriend and I always clarified who was paying what with Mother to the point she got annoyed. We didn't care. It was the only way to stay clear of her passive aggressive financial bombs.

I ended up having Ian 2 weeks past his due date. Mother had requested to be there for the birth, and ever eager to please, I saw it as a potential bonding moment with her. I suppose in some ways it was, but not enough to heal the damage she had blistered all over my very existence. She blended into the event as I went through childbirth. Ian wasn't even seven pounds when he was born. What was terrifying was seeing his blue-green lifeless body when he was born. Having the umbilical cord wrapped around his neck, he had been devoid of oxygen. I watched as the nurses worked over his limp, silent body, each moment of silence cutting through my heart. The sweetest sound was his little lungs taking their first breath as he let out the tiniest wail I ever heard. Our beautiful baby had finally arrived.

I had another child, Vinnie 5 years later. I had grown more into my own. I owned my pregnancy proudly, and never missed a moment to show off my beautiful growing belly. I loved Vinnie with the same passion as I loved Ian, and Vinnie's ears were full of singing, one-sided conversation expressing how much Vinnie was loved, and promises to do my very best. Added were the same apologies for failures I knew I would have as a parent. No parent gets out unscathed from failure in one way or another. I came to realize that's all right. It's what is done with the mistakes that are made that are the real turning and learning points. Included were words of encouragement that I would make right what I could from mistakes made.

Although she tried, I didn't let Mother's words taint me in my process of growing life the second time. I wore the two-piece bathing suit, with my big, beautiful belly hanging out for God and everyone to see at the beach. I held no shame in my growing, changing body. I had nude pregnancy photos done to remind my children that pregnancy is beautiful and should not be hidden, but cherished, and honored in its re-contouring of my body to make way for their lives.

I realized after I had my children that Mother did not have a positive experience being pregnant with me. I think she was ashamed of being pregnant, and figured because I wasn't married, that's how I should feel as well. The thing of it is, she was wrong about me. She may have tainted what I wore and how I felt about being pregnant with Ian, but she never banked on the strength of my love for Ian, and Vinnie. It was the first time I realized I was stronger than she was in my ability to overcome my circumstances and take pride in who I was.

Hope Doran

THE WEDDING

My boyfriend had asked me to marry him while I was pregnant with Ian. I joyously said yes. We were so in love and the idea of marriage was a salacious one. I had spent so many years struggling, living paycheck to paycheck, I happily welcomed his perfectionist ways. He was such a relief in my tumultuous life, and we settled into our family life of bliss.

In preparations for the wedding, I asked what I thought was a routine question. I asked Father to walk me down the aisle. I asked him while we were sitting at their home, with Mother in the room. Mother, not Father told me that would not happen. She curtly informed me Father had already done that in my first failed marriage, and he would not lower his spiritual standards and do it again, especially as I was an unmarried mother. She sarcastically said she was sure I would figure something out. Mother always knew how to emotionally crush me. I ended up asking the same dear friend who convinced me to go to John's graduation. He happily agreed to walk me down the aisle. In spite of her cutting words, she was right. I did figure it out.

We had decided on an outdoor wedding at a local B & B on West Cliff Drive. It was a beautiful day, and everything was set. I had reconnected with Cynthia, so she and her beau were in attendance. We had decided on a small wedding. Outside of family, we agreed that we both had to know everyone there, at least casually. It made for a very intimate evening.

I had gotten ready, pacing around the room. Mother knocked on the door to come in. I obliged her, opening the door to find her also dressed in white. I looked her over, the surprise I'm sure showing on my face as she told me she figured it didn't matter if she wore white, because it was not my first marriage. When I was too shocked to respond, she commented that at least it was an off shade of white as she walked out the door telling me she would see me outside. Dumbfounded, I followed in her wake down to my wedding.

The wedding was beautiful. My talented brother and some of his acquaintances provided beautiful classical music. I proudly walked down the aisle to my soon to be husband, and we were made official. A barrage of photos that were taken by our photographer followed the ceremony.

The photographers were very organized, and we blazed through the list of must-have photos. When we got to the photos with the parental units, they refused to be photographed with me directly. Instead, they stood behind me, at a distance and held hands while I was alone in the forefront. Mother really didn't miss a moment to passively tell me she disapproved.

We thought about having dancing at the wedding, but Mother had said she and Father would not participate in dancing due to religious beliefs. That being said, there would be no Father Daughter dance, or any of the other sentimental festivities in a wedding that tie people together as family. Instead, we elected to have a lovely catered dinner, cut the cake, and walk to the Santa Cruz Beach Boardwalk in our wedding attire to ride the Giant Dipper. It was a fun filled night, despite Mothers passive hostilities.

Later, when photos were ready, Mother took some, but they were never proudly displayed. More like a token of an event. When John was married some years later, the parental units danced, and danced. They proudly posed with John and his beautiful bride, Megan, for photos, and to this day, the photo of John and Megan hangs proudly in their house, for all to see. It was yet another reminder that I was not good enough to be displayed. I was more of a story that they told.

Hope Doran

UNAPPROVED SHOPPING

I made every effort to keep the parental units in our lives. I hated that I did not have a relationship with my grandmother until it was too late to flourish. I did not want that for any children I had. I ended up saying, doing, and hiding many things from the parental units as a result of the desire to see my children have a relationship with them. In hindsight, I wish I would have just kept them at a distance and been true to myself. It never occurred to me that Mother would be as cold and calculating with my children as she was with me. In my foolishness, I thought it would be different because they were her grandchildren. I learned that her narcissistic, ill behaviors didn't discriminate, at the expense of my children.

One of the ways I attempted to forge friendship with Mother was to spend time socially with her. I tried to keep things lighthearted. Hanging out with Mother started out as simple activities. Mother liked to go out and be free of her mountain home, and we would often end up meeting in town for a visit. Once again, I was thrown into the possibility that things would be different, and we would form something deep and meaningful. I gladly took the time to expand on that possibility as we did various things from the simple meeting for lunch to the more extravagant shopping adventures.

It was not a regular thing, but it was often. I enjoyed the time, and the illusion of connection. In the moment I saw it as genuine, and because of that I felt a bond to her. I came to truly enjoy these outings, and saw them as a period of growth between her and I. Because of that, they were, and continue to be some of the few cherished memories I have with Mother. Not in the spending of money, but rather the spending of time together. It was during a period where things seemed to flow easily for both of us, and I appreciated her and our seemingly budding friendship.

Another reason I enjoyed these outings so much was because I saw a more human side to Mother. Gone were the rigid, unattainable requirements. In their place was loose desire, freer conversation, and for two married women subscribing to not spending a lot of money without spousal discussion, salacious spending of money. I'm not talking car-spending expenses, just purchases we wouldn't normally do. Frankly, it was fun.

The first time it happened, I was stunned. We had gone to a larger mall that had an elite wing of such stores as Louis Vuitton, Versace, Coach, and Tiffany Co. She always wanted to visit the luxurious stores, and I went along, watching her as we perused through the high-end items she would never be prepared to purchase. Despite that, it was fun to watch her desire such things, knowing it didn't fit into either of our lives, yet still daydreaming of a world where it did. It was likely the most human experience I had with Mother, bonding over the coveting of unattainable things.

We had exited one of the stores, and I offhandedly said I had always wanted a Tiffany bracelet. Before I knew it,

Mother swung a hard left into the Tiffany store. Just like the previous one, we looked at the ornate, glimmering jewelry, and silky scarves, pretending like we would buy the store. Mother ushered me over to the bracelets and asked me which one I was talking about. I pointed to the classic, chain link, heart charm, toggle latch bracelet.

Before I realized what was happening, Mother called over an associate, asking her to retrieve the bracelet from its encasement. With a quick sweeping action, the gleaming, shiny silver was resting on my wrist. I rotated my wrist around, admiring the shiny metal, watching the Tiffany heart dangle gracefully from my arm.

I accepted its fate, took it off and returned it to the associate. Mother took it from her hands, asking how much to have it engraved. Stunned, I watched as the transaction took place. Wanting to stay silent, lest I ruin the moment. My silence was broken only when Mother wanted it engraved with my maiden name rather than my married one. When I corrected her, I saw a flash of disapproval. Her verbal response… "Oh yeah, I forgot about that," before she changed the last initial with a slight huff. In spite of the attitude, I dismissed it in the moment of receiving something from Mother that I truly wanted. It was one of the few times that happened.

On another outing we meandered around the small outdoor mall on Pacific Avenue. There was a particular antique jewelry store that became a requirement for us to frequent whenever we were in town. She was on the hunt for an upgraded wedding ring. She said that after all her years of marriage, she was entitled to it. Initially, Father had no interest in the purchase, and I can only imagine what was said behind closed doors, but eventually she won out, and Father purchased an extravagant, lavish diamond ring for her. The tragic thing is that she rarely wore it. It seemed so sad, but I think she enjoyed the fight more than the ring itself.

Mixed in with the wedding ring upgrade, Mother also had interests in other jewelry. Along the very same stretch of mall, there was another store, which offered more modern jewelry. One day she and I went in and started trying on rings. Both of us wanted to make purchases. We both knew better as far as our husbands went. So, we put them back and left.

As we perused other stores, we discussed how much we each enjoyed the rings. Mother did the unthinkable. She offered to pay for the one I liked and have me pay her back over time. For herself, she had enough money stashed away so she could also purchase the ring she enjoyed as well. It was a lovely cocktail ring comprised of rubies, sapphires, and emeralds. Mine was a simpler eternity band of small diamonds, dainty and elegant.

I asked her what she was planning on telling Father regarding her newly acquired ring. She told me she had so much jewelry she would simply refrain from wearing it for a period of time. She said later, when she decided to wear it, if Father asked her about it, she would dismissively say she had had it for a long time. I couldn't believe what I was hearing out of Mother's mouth, but her actions towards something fallible resonated with me, and I loved Mother for that, even if it was fleeting.

My ownership of the ring did not last. Years later, while I was at Mother's house, I washed my hands and accidentally left the ring on the bathroom counter. When I went back to retrieve it, there was no ring. Mother feigned looking for the ring over the next several weeks, updating me that she had opened the pipe under the sink, gone through the vacuum debris, and checked the other areas of the house with no success in finding it. I believe she secretly took the ring back for some reason. I really liked it, but could never prove what had happened, so I decided I would never make a payment arrangement with Mother again. Even on sale, the delicate ring I had paid for was over a thousand dollars.

I did finally hit my breaking point with Mother regarding going out shopping. Once again, we met up for a bite to eat, and before I knew it, Mother was telling me she wanted to go antique shopping. We loaded into my vehicle and headed to the small adjacent town of Aptos.

Mother was keen on wanting to go to one specific shop. She seemed set on a furniture purchase, saying the house furniture could use an update. We wandered around, her intent on chairs, me more browsing. Antique shopping was more Mother's wheelhouse. I was lost in thought when I heard Mother calling me from another room in the store, I sauntered over to her, watching as she was drooling over 2 Morris chairs.

I could tell immediately she wanted them. They were in pristine condition, and the price tags reflected it. The 2 chairs were being sold for over two thousand dollars. She mulled it over as I pondered how the hell, she was going to get this one past Father. I asked her that, but her mind was set, and she made the purchase.

After the purchase was complete, she panicked. It was a new side to Mother, seeing her freak out over what Father would say or do. At one point she asked if I would hold onto them. I hesitantly said yes, wondering how she planned on introducing them to Father without raising a stir even with them sitting at my house for any period of time.

After some thought, Mother decided to take the chairs home rather than have me hold them. I had the larger vehicle, so she asked me to drive them up to the house. I followed her sedan back to Bonny Doon, pulling into the long driveway I was so familiar with. Mother told me to stay outside as she went in to give Father the news.

I heard portions of the heated discussion from my vehicle and had started to pull the chairs out in an attempt to get out of there as quickly as possible. It was something new, listening to Mother's passive aggressive manipulation in an attempt to subdue Father and get what she wanted. She went on about how she never got what she wanted and didn't feel she should have to get Father's permission to make a purchase. I could not help but notice the parallels between her interactions with Father, and how she had so often interacted with me.

When Father exited the house, I could see it on his face. The silent rage filled his space as he strode up to me. We completed the task of removing the chairs and putting them into the living room in silence. Father's cheeks flushed with anger as he clenched his teeth together trying to keep his composure. I walked outside the front door and turned to say goodbye to Father. He grabbed my shoulder, and quietly told me to stay. With that, we walked back into the house.

I was there for a few hours. It was uneventful, save the hostile silence. I think Father really was so angry he needed me there, so he didn't say or do anything he regretted. When he felt it had passed, he abruptly got up, escorted me out, thanking me for staying as we walked to the vehicle.

To this day I have never seen or heard of Father sitting in either of those chairs. Whatever happened after I left must have been something fierce. That was the last time Mother ever made a purchase that excessively expensive. It has also remained the only time I ever saw her afraid of Father.

Hope Doran

AN END

After several years, my relationship ended with my husband. I was reevaluating my life, trying to make heads or tails of what I wanted, and who I really was. I felt betrayed by life. Nothing in my life was as I had been trained to believe it should be. At nearly 40 years old I felt like a failure, both in the end of another marriage and in not really knowing who I was as I defined for myself. I had spent my entire life being told what and who I should be, but that was obviously not a recipe for life that had really worked for me. I was lost.

Mother offered for Ian, Vinnie, and I to stay at the parental units' house. I agreed, thinking it would just be a few weeks while I found other housing. That plan took an abrupt turn when I lost my job. It turned out my employer had concerns regarding my new separation and didn't want to employ me any longer. Now unemployed, I began the search for any employment that would rescue my family and myself. I was unsuccessful for months in finding work. The dental field didn't want to hire me because I was too experienced, and would want more money, the fast-food chains, and retail stores saw me as a waste of time because as soon as I had a job back in the dental field, I would quit. To be fair, both were correct, but finding an office that would hire me took almost 9 months, and a pay cut, but they were the first ones that offered, and I eagerly took the position.

I was spinning out of control emotionally during those months of unemployment. I felt like a failure. I was afraid I would lose my children and found myself living back under Mother's roof. I had been spending time away from Mother's house whenever I could to ease the stress of being there. Our presence was starting to take a toll on everyone. I had never intended on living back under their roof, and it fucked with my head.

My brother's return from college for the Thanksgiving holiday was the final straw. Mother had told me I needed to find other accommodations for the holiday because John was coming, and she was giving him the room that Ian, Vinnie, and I had been sleeping in. I told her I would be back the following day to move my things.

I put off returning to the house as long as I could. John wasn't supposed to be there until the next day, so I figured it would be fine. I was wrong. I got back to the house, going up the stairs to the front door; I could see Mother looking at me through the window. I could tell she was mad. I entered, voicing a hello in an attempt at normalcy. Mother uttered a sharp hello before telling me she cleaned up the room. She proceeded to tell me it was filthy and reeked of my cheap perfume. She said things would have to be run differently after the holiday when I returned. Knowing I had kept the room clean, I was irritated by her insults, not to mention being kicked out, yet again by Mother. I sullenly went into the room to see what was left to remove for John. I opened the door to a stripped-down room, save the bed that was Mother's to begin with. The closets were also void of any clue I had inhabited the space with my 2 children.

I went back to the living room and asked Mother what she had done with our things. Without looking away from the TV, she told me my things were in the garage. I muttered thanks and went out to the garage. Once through the door, I turned the light on to survey where our things would be. I had been allowed to store some larger things in there, so I figured all our everyday items from the room would be in that area as well.

There they were, thrown into a pile. All of Ian's, Vinnie's, and my clothes had been shoved into an old dog crate, with the overflow on top. Shoes were thrown into a bag and tossed on top of that, some falling out onto the floor. She had successfully eliminated me out of the house. All of our clothes now smelled like a dirty, stale dog. She single-handedly managed to convey that I was worthless to her in the process of "cleaning" my things up.

I packed my things, shoving them into every dark crack and crevice I could inside my vehicle. I did not say goodbye. I left in tears. Once again, Mother had effectively let me know I was someone to tolerate, but never really love. I never stayed the night there again. Later, Mother asked why I didn't come back. I told her she hurt my feelings by shoving our clothes into the dirty, stinky dog kennel and tossing the rest around like my things were just something to discard. Her response was cold. She said, "Well, it was the best space to keep them all together." She never apologized, but in hindsight, I really don't think she thought she did anything wrong because doing me a favor to her meant I lost control. In that, she could do and say what she wanted regarding me, and I should have just shut up, been grateful even if she was nasty about it.

THOSE PEOPLE

One of the biggest changes to my life came as a torpedo of a revelation. I was gay. Not the gay as in happy, but the gay as in the one that Pentecostal Christians such as Mother, hated. I had always found myself attracted to women, but figured it was for the female form and not a true physical attraction. In the stillness of seeking out what I needed to love myself, to feel free, to be successful, and honest, I acknowledged what was my truth. It went against absolutely everything I had been brought up believing. There it was anyway, despite massive amounts of counseling, and church indoctrination. I had never felt such a freedom and fear as when I finally acknowledged my reality. But acknowledging and accepting are two different things. An inability, or unwillingness to accept who I really was, almost cost me my life…again.

I was in a very passionate relationship with a woman. She was the first woman I had ever had a sexual relationship with. She ignited a sensual passion in me I did not know I had. She was unlike anyone I had ever met. She was bold, and although barely 5'2" tall, walked like she owned the world. She was very intelligent, with soulful green eyes that mesmerized me, and orange-red hair that fit her fiery personality. I felt like she saw me for who I was and loved me right where I was at. She helped me to see outside the heterosexual box I had been confined in all my years, and I loved her for that.

I didn't know it until I was immersed in loving her, but she had her own demons she was battling. Between the two of us, we didn't stand a chance. She grew irritated that I wouldn't just tell Mother to fuck off and that I was gay. It became a contentious rift between us. My fear of Mother's reprisal over being gay kept me frozen in terror with regards to my relationships with both Mother and my girlfriend. The struggles that my girlfriend was facing compounded our situation, and because of that I don't think she ever understood where I was really at within my own hell.

I had begun cutting as a way of clearing my head. It filled the space with something I was in control of, and that had a soothing quality to it. My own clouded perception of where I was bled into my girlfriend's struggles. The cutting continued over the months as we fought continually over our demons rather than trying to support and help each other. Each of us thought the other's struggles could be fixed so simply, not fully seeing the complexity of either one. She would rage at me through the bathroom door when I retreated there in an attempt to find some semblance of center in cutting. The ringing in my ears as I sliced through the tender skin of my arm helped silence her, as well as the voices in my head, if only for the moment.

I reached my darkest point regarding being gay one day, when I was visiting Mother. I had been talking about playing softball, and how much fun I was having, regaling her with the antics of the last game I had played. Mother cut me off to tell me one of her friends from church had seen me holding hands with a girl, and kissing. I sat back in awe of how quickly she could turn a lighthearted conversation into an attack. I also knew I was too paranoid to hold my girlfriend's hand in public, let alone kiss her, so I knew Mother was lying. I didn't trust her enough to have an honest conversation about being gay, so I simply told her that her friend was wrong.

Mother continued, unhindered by my response. She said it was probably just a mistake (emphasis on probably). She went on to exclaim that she had absolutely no idea what I could possibly have in common with *those people,* referring to anyone who was gay. She continued to barrage me with how ungodly it was to be gay, and how all the gay people would rot in hell for turning away from God. The final coup de grace was when she buttoned up her tirade by informing me that there was absolutely no room for *those people* in her life, and she would disown anyone who told her they were gay.

I felt the air leave my lungs as I slowly exhaled, not realizing I had been holding my breath. There it was, her final answer. I don't think I had ever been so relieved to have kept my mouth shut as I did in that moment. I knew my children would lose whatever relationship they had with Mother should she ever find out. Not realizing at the time, but they were destined to have the same relationship I had had with her my entire life. We parted ways, and I sat in my car processing my now more definitive reality. To be honest with Mother would be to lose all hope of ever having what I wanted with her.

When I returned to my girlfriend's house, I told her what happened. I was hoping for support, but mixed with her own hell she was facing, we found ourselves quickly fighting. I retreated to the bathroom in a depressive rage. She was outside the door trying to get in, but I had wedged my body between the door and the counter, making entrance impossible. She hit the door before retreating, and I was left in silence, save the voices raging in my head.

I started with my usual spot for cutting. I could feel the depression settle like a heavy cloak around me. The razor dropped to the floor as my body became so heavy with helplessness I was lost in desperation. I felt like I did not fit in anywhere. I felt useless, I felt unloved. I felt like a shell of a human devoid of any worth. I felt like I had faked my entire life and would have to continue to do so in order to survive. I was so tired of all these feelings and emotions that had lived in my head, heart, and soul for my entire life. I wanted it over. I wanted to be released from all these demons of inadequacy that seeped into every relationship I had.

I picked the razor back up and let its tip rest on an old wound. As I proceeded to push deeper into the scar that I had given myself so many years earlier, I was gifted with the clarity of a reason to live. My children. I paused as I realized the impact of my decision on their lives. What it would do to them emotionally. I didn't want my self-inflicted death to be something that resonated throughout their entire lives. I still felt the weighty emotion of depression, and helplessness, but the love for my children gave me enough light to see past the moment of the overwhelming feeling of worthlessness.

That was the beginning of the end with my first female love. I saw we were toxic to each other. I couldn't see a way through me accepting I was gay, and owning who I was with Mother while I watched my girlfriend entangled within her own struggle. I knew as much as I wanted to, I couldn't take on her demons, nor was I in a space to help her. She, likewise, couldn't see a way to ease my troubled soul. The road out of that relationship was a rocky one, embedded with love, passion, hate, and frustration. But in the end, I believe it was what we both needed to grow and change.

Hope Doran

SPANKING

After those 9 long months of unemployment, it was so, so good to be back into work. It helped a lot with my feeling of self-worth. During some of my longer days, Mother would occasionally ask to take Vinnie or Ian to spend some time together. The kids always seemed to enjoy the time, so I gladly said yes.

Things seemed to go okay for some time. As Ian got older, he started to gravitate more towards spending time with Father, which seemed natural. Unfortunately, I think Mother did not like being second fiddle as Ian and Father began to have a more regular hang out routine. Mother eventually quit including Ian, and began to spend time with Vinnie alone, but would often complain of Vinnie's antics.

Vinnie was always a handful. I don't ever remember a time that was different. Vinnie always looked up to Ian, who was always very well behaved and driven in his life's adventures. Vinnie took notice of the stark differences between them, and at one point asked me if it was okay to not know what they wanted to do with their life. I said absolutely. Vinnie followed that by asking if it was okay that they were so different from Ian. I said it was and told Vinnie that they would likely see so much more of the world than any of us because they chose to challenge it.

I always saw that as a beautiful feature of Vinnie, and thought Vinnie would do great things, and facilitate dramatic change in having the mentality of challenging the system. I would often tell Vinnie I thought great things were in store for them. Privately, I also knew that getting Vinnie honed in on the skill of challenging perspective with respect rather than brazen righteous fury was going to be formidable as a parent. Nevertheless, I gladly took it on seeing the bigger picture. Vinnie's mentality towards the world was difficult for anyone to navigate, but especially challenging for Mother.

Mother had asked to spend some time with Vinnie. Towards the end of the day, I drove out to pick Vinnie up from Mother's house. It was a lovely spring day, and I imagined they had a good time doing one of the many activities Mother had spoken of embarking on with Vinnie. When I arrived, I trotted up the stairs and into Mother's home, only to find Vinnie on the couch, sullen and in a flat mood. I asked what was wrong, but got no response back, so I went to find Mother, who was in the kitchen.

Mother proceeded to tell me that Vinnie's attitude sucked. She said Vinnie was ungrateful and needed to be put in their place. She followed with saying she thought it was important that Vinnie knew they didn't rule the roost, and my parenting needed to improve. I asked Mother what happened, and she said "everything" with an exasperated snort. She went on to say it was a good thing I got there when I did because she was getting ready to spank Vinnie and had told Vinnie she would.

My heart dropped. Now I understood why Vinnie was so sullen. She had the same look I'm sure I wore so very many times throughout my childhood. For a moment, I was that same little girl that was terrified of her mother. Knowing a spanking was Mother's translation for beating, I panicked. I thought about all the times I had been beaten, and how it had only served to terrify me of the parental units, and later, just pissed me off. I shook my head in shock, looked Mother in the eye, and told her she would never have to worry about being so vexed with regards to Vinnie again.

I retreated to the living room and collected Vinnie off the couch. We left the house hand in hand. I got Vinnie settled into the car and we drove off. I asked Vinnie what happened, and Vinnie told me Mother had offered several things to do, and Vinnie had made the mistake of telling Mother the idea of hiking around the home was boring.

Vinnie admitted copping an attitude with Mother, and knew it wasn't acceptable. We discussed boundaries, politeness, and respect, which were frequent conversations we shared. I was of the opinion that a "spanking" was not the correct response to the situation and was glad I had arrived when I did. Out of my outright refusal to allow Mother's abuse to become multi-generational, Vinnie was never left alone with Mother again.

Hope Doran

THE BLANKET

During my time of unemployment, I had been going completely stir crazy. I needed something to do, so I dove into the creative side of myself, and took up crafting. The first thing I made was a crocheted blanket for Vinnie. It had wild colors of Vinnie's choosing and it fit Vinnie's personality. For a beginner, it was complex, and I was so proud of the blanket when it was done. Even more so, I loved how much it meant to Vinnie.

Over time I had gone on to make several blankets for people who were dear to me. They all varied in flawed beauty, and I enjoyed creating each of them. I had moved from crochet to rudimentary quilting and loved the results. Everyone seemed to thoroughly enjoy my efforts, and it felt good taking the time to show people I cared about them.

One of my favorite blankets was one I made as a Christmas gift. My employer created these savvy games each holiday season for all the employees. We all looked forward to what would be unveiled as the Christmas game. When we received the rules for the latest one, we were a bit stumped.

We were each given a dollar, and then drew names. Whoever's name we drew, that's who we were then tasked to find and purchase a meaningful gift for. The caveat was that the gift could not exceed the one-dollar price point. Then, at the dinner, we were to present the gift, and explain why we chose it for them. None of us were really thrilled with the game. I understood the principle behind it. I saw the point being to discuss that the individual was where the true value lied, and the gift was subsequent. But along with that lesson was the idea that there was a difference between knowing what someone would like versus purchasing a meaningful gift with only a dollar. The game seemed somewhat contradictory.

My rebellious streak raised her head as I pondered what I could gift my sweet co-worker. I would not have done this for just any of my co-workers, but I considered her a friend as well, and wanted to give something that fit the criteria, but was truly special. She was pregnant at the time, and I thought that a lap blanket would be something I could complete in the short amount of time I had. I gathered all the remnants of fabric I had collected from the previous projects I had completed and set to work on a beautiful throw blanket. I only had 3 days to complete my project. Because of that, I was up late every night after I got off work, laying out the blanket on the floor as I pinned everything together. The final product was beautiful. I boxed it up and wrapped it. Seeing that I didn't pay anything for the blanket I made, I turned the dollar bill into the ribbon.

We all arrived for the party. Everyone with small trinket packages, save mine. Everyone wanted to know whom I had drawn. We each took turns pretending to enjoy the gifts we received. To be fair, everyone at least knew the person they had drawn well enough to manage a gift along likable lines. When it was my turn to present, I handed over my gift. Her jaw dropped when she opened it to see my beautiful creation, along with everyone else. There was a lot of oohing and awing over it. Others were saying they wished I had drawn them instead. I was glad I had gifted her the blanket, but I did not gain favor with my boss, who saw it as grossly unfair, even though I did stay within her parameters.

I told Mother about the Christmas party and my gifting of a handmade quilt. She retorted with asking why I never made her one. She said it seemed like I had made everyone else one. Surprised by her response, I told her I didn't think she would be interested in having one. She informed me I was wrong and asked that I make her a quilt, so I said I would.

Then the demands started. Mother excused herself and came out a few minutes later with remnants of fabric from her bedroom curtains. She asked me to incorporate the material into the quilt to tie everything together. I liked the idea, and gladly took the material. Seeing that I was unfazed, she then proceeded to tell me that she wanted the quilt I made to be floor length for three sides of her California King bed.

In spite of not having the space to make something on such a grand scale, I said okay. Seeming to continue in seeking a reaction, she told me she wanted heavy green colors, and nothing too busy, like some of the other blankets I had made. Within a few minutes, the happiness over making something nice for Mother had turned into a massive chore. I did not let it show though. I was not going to give her the satisfaction.

Undaunted, I took on the task. I changed my mindset to take the project on as a challenge. Mother knew the limited space I had to work with, which just made the project that much more over the top and ridiculous. It made me wonder if she had been trying to set me up for failure. I decided there was no room for failure as I started on the massive quilt. I did sections at a time (keep in mind I never took a quilting class, I only made blankets as a way to channel some creative energy due to boredom). I made slow progress with the massive blanket, but really enjoyed how it was coming along. It took months to finish but oh, how I loved the final product! It was a stunning piece of work, and I was really proud of the outcome. I had measured it several times to make sure it fit Mother's criteria of going all the way to the floor of her massive bed.

When I presented it to her, she looked it over, said it was nice and thanked me. I had to ask her to put it on the bed so I could see how my final product looked in her room. She complied, and we assembled the quilt on the bed. It was perfect. It was also the last time I ever saw the quilt.

Later on, I asked her about the quilt. She shrugged it off saying it was too heavy for her and she couldn't use it. I asked if I could have it back if it was something she wasn't going to use. I told her I would make something lighter in its place. She flatly said no. I was crushed. All of my hard work was shoved away in the back of some closet, or in a box somewhere. Wasted away for lack of love, just like I was in Mother's eyes.

IT'S BETTER THAN A HOUSE!

It was early in spring when we started hearing mumblings from Mother. She was working on a Christmas gift for John and I. She was very excited about the gift, and rarely missed a moment to mention it in one way or another. She had a history of disappointing us, so for me, I was very passive in my responses.

My lack of interest seemed to annoy Mother. She started to talk more about it. She would say things like, it was a big deal, or point out that it was taking a lot of planning and coordinating. All of this fell on uninterested ears. Still, she continued ranting and raving over it for months, all with passive reception from both John and myself.

It was really hard for us to become excited over gifts Mother gave. Especially when she made such a big point out of how much it would be enjoyed by the recipient. John and I had both been in similar situations and had ended up sorely disappointed by her fanfare. We would discuss the situation, and through conversation, began to think perhaps for once it really was a wonderful, exciting gift. I foolishly began to get excited as we began to ponder all the bigger things Mother had spoken about doing throughout our lives. One thing that resonated was that she had always wanted to go to Ireland. We thought maybe, just maybe it would be a family trip. That was something that would take a lot of planning, and something Mother would be excited for.

I held this excitement cautiously close to myself when Mother spoke about it. I would be lying if I said I didn't get a little more excited every time Mother brought up the gift. The months progressed quickly, woven in and out of Mother's boasting about the gift, and I found myself excited for Christmas, in spite of myself. It was the first Christmas in a really long time that I was looking forward to as far as gifts went. In my daydreams, if the gift was a grand trip, all of us would be going, and I pondered what a trip with all of us would look like. I wasn't the only one who had concluded it was a trip. Literally everyone I spoke with about it mirrored the same thought, and John was in wistful agreement as well.

While talking to Mother on the phone, she started to talk about the gift. In the flurry of her excitement, she exclaimed that it was better than a house! I couldn't believe what I was hearing. With the holiday coming down to the wire, I knew it was all bullshit. Whatever it was would most certainly not be what I had been daydreaming about. John and I discussed it and found the whole thing humorous at this point. We had both drawn the conclusion that nothing we had come up with in our wild, imaginative thoughts would have been better than a house. Especially seeing as neither of us owned a house at that point.

Rather than being irritated over it, we began to banter about it, taking turns joking around as we pretended to receive the gift. We practiced all the different ways we would feign excitement over such a lavish gift. We laughed about it, putting fun into the gift that was most assuredly not better than a house. It ended up being a blessed gift of laughter in its pre-gifting status.

I was at the house visiting, and Mother had begun her boasting about the magical Christmas gift that had become larger than life. Mid-sentence she paused, pondered for a moment before stating perhaps she exaggerated when she was talking about how great her gift was. "No shit," I said in my inside voice, while smiling demurely, telling her I was sure we would love it.

We knew there was no way we would perceive the gift as something as grand as Mother had made it out to be. John and I began in earnest practicing faces of surprise and gratitude. We had decided to treat it as we would any other holiday and receive it from a space of being grateful for the gift just as it was, no matter what it was. After all, Mother had obviously gone to some sort of great lengths to prepare it.

Before we knew it, the holiday was upon us. We always spent Christmas at the parental unit's home. It was tradition. That, and they would rarely come to either of our houses for the Christmas holiday. The smell of fresh coffee permitted their home as we walked through the door, the kids in tow with all their wide-eyed excitement. The tree was in its full glory, all lit up and decorated with Mother's large array of beautiful bird ornaments. We all gathered around and enjoyed each other's company, while sipping morning coffee and devouring delicious pastries. I had learned to enjoy Christmas for the beauty of its lights, decorations, and the feeling of family over the giving of the gifts. So, as the gift giving began, I didn't mind the painfully slow pace that things progressed at for the sake of "extending the excitement," as Mother would say.

It was no surprise to either John or I that Mother saved the "big" gift for the finale. It was her way of doing things. She handed John and I our gifts at the same time and told us to open them simultaneously. We obliged her, and each opened a heavy-laden, 3-inch binder filled to the max with papers. We looked at each other, trying to take in what it was. Both of us were perplexed.

"It's your genealogy," Mother squealed with delight! We slowly absorbed what she was saying. She went on to tell us she had used two different companies to cross check the information to ensure it was as complete and accurate as possible. There were copies of photos of our long-lost ancestors attached to various family trees. Along with the binder were books that fit into our genealogy as well. It was a cool gift, and we both gushed over it for what it was. Later, John and I spoke of all the hype leading up to the event and agreed it didn't come close to home ownership. For the life of us, we couldn't understand how the hell she figured that two individuals who did not own a home would concur that it was better than a house. We still joke about it to this day.

In our lighthearted banter later in life, we had a discussion regarding why she would go to such lengths and say such extravagant things regarding our genealogy. It seemed to us that Mother had been seeking to escape her old, dilapidated Bonny Doon home for years before that dream finally came true. The observation we both agreed on was that despite the move to the house she wanted, Mother seemed to have been lacking in excitement over her new home. Between whatever internal battles she was having regarding the house, it seemed compounded by a crisis of self-identity. We think she pursued our genealogy as a way of finding that inner peace, and her ability to obtain her identity through the genealogy research was better than any house she could ever have.

What Mother failed to realize was that we didn't have the same internal struggles that we believe she battled. She placed her identity in a different space than either of us. So, while her gift was a lovely one, it was just that for us. I paused for a moment, taking in our conversation, and marveled that in spite of all of my life's struggles, I was still able to say I was more at peace then Mother perhaps ever was. In that moment I felt sorry for the mother I never had.

Hope Doran

THE CUTTING BOARD

For the longest time, holidays were celebrated at the parental unit's home. Such celebrations were usually low key, regardless of what holiday it was. We would all gather and converse, play games or help food prep for lunch or dinner. It was usually a pretty good time with John, Megan, Ian, Vinnie, and myself.

There had been almost a ritual of sorts attached to these events. When it came to meal prep, I was always in charge of cutting or dicing things up. For as long as I could remember, that was my job. Every time I would go to do said job, I was given one cutting board. It was the one they had used to beat me with all those years earlier. Even if I grabbed another one, Mother would replace it with that one, giving one lame excuse or another for the switch.

The board was old and had a split up the face of it. I recalled that split originating on my ass from the last time I was hit with it. I spent my time doing my assigned chore sullen as I made deep score marks into the faded wood, wishing it was not put forth as a constant reminder of the pain that it dealt out in my youth. It was Mother's passive aggressive reminder to me of all the intimate encounters my ass and legs had with the broken board as a result of not being good enough.

The old piece of wood from days gone by served as a constant reminder that although I was in their house, being present came with a price. It was handed to me as a place card, serving as a reminder that things were not as good as they may have seemed in the holiday moments. The board was really more useless than helpful, except as the remembrance. I knew what Mother was doing. I hated that she incorporated that into our gatherings.

Thanksgiving was coming, and I had made a decision. I was done being hit emotionally with that cutting board. I despised even touching the old board. It had an incredibly negative energy attached to it that affected me for days. I decided this was the last holiday anyone; especially me, was going to use the fractured old piece of wood.

I packed up for the short drive as I normally would. The only change I made was to switch out my purse for the biggest one I had. I wanted to be sure I could zip up the bag so nothing would be discovered. I packed us into the car, and we were off to their house.

When the time came, I gladly accepted the cutting board. Invigorated from the energy of my plan, I set to work on my chopping task. When I was done, I offered to clean up the kitchen from the meal prep while everyone else went into the living room. I had strategically placed my purse in the kitchen so I would be ready to put my plan into action. I busied myself with cleaning, starting with the cutting board. I washed and dried it before sliding it into my bag and zipping it closed. I finished the kitchen, and joined the family in the living room, casually putting my purse by the door.

The missing cutting board was left undetected, and I enjoyed my Thanksgiving celebration. I felt light as air knowing that after the end of the night, I would never have to hold that awful reminder of my past again. I was practically giddy.

I returned back to my house. I had told my girlfriend at the time about my plan. She and her sister joined me in my true Thanksgiving celebration. We lit a fire in our backyard fire pit. We all sat around, drinking, and celebrating my singular act of setting myself free from a piece of my past. I grabbed my camera and pulled the cutting board out of my purse. I very deliberately placed the board into the flames. As I watched the fire begin to sear the old cutting board, I took a moment, giving thanks for finally setting a piece of my childhood free in the flames. I commemorated the celebration by taking a series of photos during the fiery destruction of the cutting board.

I sat by the fire pit long past the death of the flames. I watched as the embers faded into dusty ash feeling a little bit freer. I smiled to myself, wondering if Mother would ever comment on the missing cutting board. She never did. To complete my plan, I printed one of the photos onto a large canvas that has hung proudly in my home every day since, serving as a reminder to me that I am not the sum of my past.

Hope Doran

KOSHI

One pet or another always surrounded me during my entire existence. I loved animals, whether they were mine, or someone else's. I had reached a point in my life when I did not have any animals, but my girlfriend at the time had a sweet boxer dog. Daisy was an amazing dog. She always followed my girlfriend around, wanting her attention constantly. Daisy had found her human. I loved Daisy but realized that I wanted a dog of my own. I had never had a dog that was just my dog, and likewise, I was their human. It was a relationship I had always coveted, whether it was one of Mother's many dogs, any previous partner's dog, or the relationship Daisy and my girlfriend shared.

There had been many dogs in my life, but for one reason or another they became imprinted to someone else. Because of that, I wanted to choose my dog wisely, so I started doing research into dog's temperaments. Initially, I wanted a smaller dog. My girlfriend detested the idea of a smaller dog, so I switched gears and put a deposit down on a Newfoundland puppy to make her happy. However, the more I thought about it, the less I liked the idea of having a dog of that size. I was not a homeowner, so I saw it as a potentially difficult situation being a renter, even in the house we were currently in. I decided that if it was to be my dog, I should get what I wanted. With that, I put a deposit down on a Mini Australian Shepherd instead.

My decision was not well received. I didn't care. I had always gone to great lengths to meet her needs and desires. I realized I had spent most of my life trying to make other people happy, and I had noticed I neglected myself, and what I wanted time after time. I stuck to my decision, and my girlfriend said, "Whatever, it's your dog anyway." I agreed, and eagerly waited for the day when I could bring my puppy home.

The only other time I was that excited about an animal was when I was a child and had captured a feral cat. I had been told by Father to go try to catch the cat to get me out of the house. I asked if I could keep the cat if I caught it, and he had offhandedly said, "Yeah, sure."

I spent hours chasing that poor black kitten around the outside of the house. When the black ball of fur dove under the house to hide, I braved going under the house. I had never gone under the house before. It was dark and faded into an inky black haze as I tried to see within its belly. There were also huge spiders that made their presence known with thick webs that cascaded across the entrance.

Knowing the small kitten was under there, I stood at the entrance jumping in small circles while flailing my arms, trying to summon up enough courage to push through the sticky, massive webs. Finally, I dove in, wiggled around on my tummy, as I wormed my way deeper under the house. I shuffled around in the darkness as my eyes adjusted to the light. I wiggled from one corner to another until I had the poor kitten cornered. I reached out, grabbed him, and pulled him to my chest, tucking him under my neck as I shimmied my way out. The kitten was terrified, and by the time I retreated out from under the house, I was filthy, scratched, and bloody. I ran into the house and announced that I had caught the cat.

Mother did not want another cat and was telling me that I needed to put the kitten back outside. I told her that Father had said I could keep it. Mother's gaze shifted past me to where Father was standing. Her eyes narrowed as she asked him if this was correct, and he confirmed that it was. She said, "Fine, then I get to name the cat."

Mother named the cat Koshka. She said it meant cat in Croatian. I came to find out it was actually Russian for cat. We called him Koshi for short. I was his human from the start, which irritated Mother. Because of that, Mother charged me with cleaning up after all the cats. She said if I wanted one so bad, I could take care of them all. I didn't care. It was one of a handful of fond memories from childhood. I named my puppy Koshi in that remembrance.

When I finally got my puppy home, I was beside myself. Koshi was everything I wanted, and my girlfriend's lack of interest in him made it easy for him to bond with me. I took some time off work and within the few days I had, my sweet puppy was potty trained. He followed me everywhere. My heart melted knowing I finally got my wish. I was his human.

When the time came to go back to work, my boss let me keep Koshi kenneled under my desk as long as he was quiet. It was done as a trial, but Koshi was such a good puppy it was never a problem. Even from such a young age, it was more important for Koshi to be with me then free from the kennel. This only served to further bond us together.

Years passed, and I realized the end of my relationship with my girlfriend. I had started looking for housing in June, but having changed jobs to something part time, I did not make as much money as I used to. I attempted to juggle looking for a new job, helping my dear friend Cynthia through a crisis of her own, and looking for housing all without tipping my hand that I was getting ready to physically leave the relationship that had emotionally ended months earlier.

However, setting myself up was not an easy task. I was yet again trying to find employment as a well-seasoned worker, against others who were newer in the dental field, and would happily take a lower wage. The rental requirements were outrageous for the Santa Cruz area, and I was working against the fact I had my beloved Koshi. Despite my concerted efforts, I was struggling.

I had told Mother I was looking for housing. Of course, I asked for help under the pretense of anything other than the breakup from my girlfriend. She would offer the occasional housing possibilities she would see, which I would check out; only to find they did not accept pets. She grew irritated as Koshi became a frequent reason, along with finances for being denied housing. At one point she flatly said I should just get rid of the damn dog so I could get into a place. I told her I loved Koshi and wouldn't do that. She asked if I loved the dog more than having a home for the kids and me. I sharply retorted that my finances were the other part of the equation, and it wasn't just about the dog. I clarified that I would find housing for all of us because we were a family, and it wasn't just about Koshi.

Mother grew tired of the conversation, and eventually just stopped volunteering information. I was grateful. I didn't understand how it would cross her mind to get rid of a beloved pet. Then I realized something. She was completely willing to get rid of me, so of course, a dog was nothing more than something that served a purpose, and when it no longer fit, became disposable.

Thankfully Koshi was more than that to me. He had bonded with me so strongly; I don't think he would have survived new ownership. To Mother, Koshi was nothing more than a hindrance, so she never saw his attachment as an issue but thankfully, it was not her decision to make. Housing eventually happened for me, and I was always thankful that I did not allow Mother's insistence of dumping the dog affect my decision to keep him. We ended up enjoying years and years of time with our sweet Koshi.

Hope Doran

OFFICIAL

In the throes of trying to find housing for my family, I met Alisa. We had mutual friends that thought we would make a good pair. They encouraged Alisa to come out to a softball game and meet me. All of this was without my knowing, so Alisa had an easy out with no commitment.

I was instantly drawn to Alisa, without knowing she was there to actually meet me. We made casual conversation, and I immediately wondered how I could spend more time with her. She commanded attention, was witty as all get out, and oh baby, was she hot! Without knowing anything about her, I oddly felt like I knew her, and that intrigued me.

The road to us being together was rough. She had recently left a long-term relationship, and I was in the throes of exiting mine. At one point she even told me to not contact her. I was crushed but honored her request. Time passed and I could not get her out of my head. I missed the person I didn't really know. I told this to a friend who suggested I reach out to her. I repeated that Alisa had said not to contact her, and my friend said, 'Well then what do you have to lose?" On the advice of my friend, I brazenly called Alisa.

Apparently, I had waited just long enough for Alisa to be willing to take my call. We talked about so many things that day. Places we had been, things we had tried, jobs we had, and things we wanted to do. At one point in the conversation, I called her a Jill of all trades, because she had done and accomplished so many varying things in her life. She flippantly said she would try anything once. I told her if she was willing to try anything once, then she should try me. The momentary silence was excruciating, but she broke it by saying she was a person of her word and would meet me for ice cream.

I was nervous as all get out the day of our non-date. I got to the tiny Penny Ice Creamery early so I could get one of the few outdoor seats they had. I didn't know what car she drove, so I had no warning when she made the turn, and I was face to face with her. She would later tell me that I lit up like a Christmas tree, and she knew she was in trouble. We ended up walking around, and ice cream turned into food and drinks. By the end of the day, we were both smitten.

As days turned to months, my love for Alisa grew quickly. She was hesitant, but I could tell she was growing in love with me as well. She and I were a match unlike anything I had ever encountered. As time progressed, I knew she would be the person that was worth the loss of any relationship with Mother. I contemplated how I would have this conversation and prepared myself for the inevitable consequences Mother had so clearly defined.

My wait was not long. I had just gotten off work when my brother called to tell me Mother called him to ask if he knew I was gay. I panicked. I had really wanted my information to be presented on my terms, but that was stripped from me. I had been outed by my child. I don't know if it was done out of spite, anger, frustration, or out of some sort of retaliation towards the life changes I had made. Whatever the reason, my secret was spoken, and my power taken from me and held by someone else I loved. I couldn't retaliate. To do so would have meant losing yet another relationship. I was not willing to make that sacrifice, no matter how much I lost in the disclosure.

I hung up with John and called Mother to feel out my new situation. The moment she answered, I could tell it would be as she had predicted so many times before. She didn't want to talk to me. She proceeded to tell me the plans Ian and Father had for later in the week were canceled. She continued with canceling plans she and I had. I sat in my car listening to her, feeling her relief through the phone. She was setting herself free from me. No more obligatory love towards me. All of it, canceled for being gay. I told her I loved her, and she hung up on me.

I consoled myself with the fact that I was already planning on telling Mother. Alisa was so extraordinary as a human, and as a girlfriend. She ignited in me a passion to be true to who I was. I learned from her that in being true to myself, I would be able to live my life without the fear that had held me hostage for so many years.

Mother held true to her word. She has never really spoken to me again; save a few responses to texts I would send her. I still held onto the possibility perhaps something would change in her. After her blatant absence from all our major life events, I finally found the space to say our relationship was gone. It was more than gone, but it would be one last rejection from her, years later before I knew the death of my relationship with my mother. It would leave my heart oddly broken and healed at the same time.

ALISA

If you're lucky, you have moments with individuals who you have an instant connection with. Those people you feel you have known all your life even though you just met them. People that conjure up the belief in past lives because there could be no way for you to feel the way you did about them without having had a soul altering life with them before. They make you believe in soul mates, true love, and the ability to call them home. Those individuals alter who you are simply by their presence. It's as if your universe finally aligns itself, and everything within you finds a space of peace.

Alisa was, and continues to be, my magic. She was my match from go. It wasn't that I loved her instantly, but I was drawn to her as if I had been searching for her throughout my life, and finally found her. I had an intense feeling that I shouldn't lose sight of her, and if I did, I would never be the same. There was an odd sadness over the mere idea of her not being present in my life, even though she wasn't really in my life at that point. For that reason, I sought after her, and we grew to find love and peace within each other's lives.

From the very beginning, we were unfazed in our union. We loved what we were doing and the fact that we were a true team. From go I supported her fostering her nephew. Later we rallied together to become guardians to her niece, both due to the crisis of Alisa's sister. We bound our blended family together, offering our love freely, seeking to meet our kids right where they were. We understood this was a monumental change for everyone.

We disregarded the perpetual hate that the parental units tried to oppress us with. We found our way through financial, housing, and emotional rollercoasters. We have held each other in strong, loving support through the deaths of loved ones that broke our hearts. We navigated through the business of society to find better ways to live the lives we have been given. We have found pathways to peace with what we cannot change.

Alisa has been my champion. Through the years we have become a powerful force within our relationship and grown within its love. Speaking for myself, I would not be the person I am today without her nurturing spirit. She has been an inspiration to me in so many ways and has supported me through my life's journey. Through the times when I reached out to Mother, even knowing her response, Alisa would support me and ease my heartache over Mother's continued rejection.

Alisa did more than that though. She didn't reject them. Despite everything, she continued in her kindness, for my sake. When Father came alone to Ian and Vinnie's graduations, Alisa was welcoming. When celebrations were held at our home for those events, Alisa welcomed Father into our home, knowing full well she would never be welcome in his. She was bigger than the sum of the situation, and it made me love her even more.

Alisa has been nothing but loving and supportive. She was my rock while I set out and achieved my college degree.

She has been a sounding board for all of my hopes and dreams, as well as a shoulder to cry on when my dream of having a mom was obliterated. She has always been there for me without question, and without reservation. She is the best I could have ever hoped for in a partner. I could not be more grateful that I broke through the heartache and pain Mother had painted into my life to see I was worth such fantastic love.

I stand by what I said; Alisa was worth the loss of the parental units. What I had with them wasn't real anyway. It was a shell of perception that allowed me to interact with them. My facade helped Ian and Vinnie maintain a relationship with them a little bit longer. I had hoped it would be different for my children, but deep down, I knew it would end up being the same as it was for me. I knew Mother's love (if you could call it that) would be conditional. I guess I just wanted better for them, so I continued despite what I knew was truth.

Alisa helped me with unwavering patience as I navigated through the emotional loss of my parents. She instilled in me what the parental units should have, which was the fact that I was beautiful just as I was. She completed a lesson I had already begun to learn. I do not need to change who I truly am for acceptance. If someone does not accept me, they are not worth my efforts. I don't need to fit someone else's idea of who or what I should be to be loved, and as such I was worth loving exactly how I came. I finally removed all the ugliness that Mother had painted into my life. Alisa patiently helped me find my new canvas, and I began to paint my beautiful world, as I believed it should be.

MEETING MOTHER

The invitation came to us along with the disclaimer that everyone was invited. I'm sure Mother got the same disclaimer, but I didn't care. I had reached a point where I preferred to challenge Mother with my presence then pine over a non-existent relationship. So, when John and Megan sent out a housewarming invitation, I happily replied we would all be attending.

The day of their party was beautiful. Alisa drove us through blissful sunlight out to John and Megan's new Watsonville home. We unloaded ourselves and happily trounced into the house. I recall thinking how exciting it was for them to have a place to call theirs and create new memories within its walls. The party was a potluck, so we all brought some form of deliciousness, and I added ours to the table and went towards the side patio, where most everyone had begun to gather. I girded my loins in preparation for seeing Mother and stepped outside into the wonderful afternoon air. I felt her eyes on me before I saw her. By the time I turned to look, she was back to looking elsewhere, attempting to be aloof. That was fine by me, because it took a moment for me to register how incredibly frail she looked. She had evaporated into a ghost of the person she was in my mind, and looked as though even breathing was a difficulty. I marveled over how much damage a few years could render. I marveled over how someone who had seemed so powerful to me could end up being so brittle. She had become a paper dragon. Burned by her own flame.

As I stood there, I observed it was the first time I had been in her presence when she seemed socially awkward and uncomfortable. I'd be lying if I said that didn't please me on some level. It was about time she felt uncomfortable sitting in a situation of her own doing. Still, being the codependent person I was, politely gave her frail body a hug and sat down beside her.

Our conversation, if you could call it that, was painfully forced. Mixed in with awkward silence, was her decision to ignore questions or comments I was making. It had gotten to the point where it was almost comical. Vinnie coming up to Mother and saying hello interrupted our clumsy interaction.

Mother looked at Vinnie, and proceeded to say, "Oh, you must be Alisa, how nice to meet you." Vinnie and I looked at each other and started laughing. It had been many years since Mother had seen Vinnie, but Vinnie still looked like Vinnie. In that moment I silently observed Mother hadn't lost her passive aggressive bullshit game. She was looking to make me feel awkward and embarrass me, but she fell flat. I didn't care, and it showed. She looked at me for a reaction, but not getting what she wanted, she grew irritated. It was a moment when I observed that without realizing it, I truly had begun to reclaim my power, and love who I was.

Alisa had come in behind Vinnie, and I introduced Alisa to Mother. Alisa tried to converse with Mother, but Mother was too busy trying to regain control of a situation she never had control of in the first place. Mother resorted to ignoring me completely and pretended she couldn't hear what Alisa was saying. We tired of her antics and left her alone. Shortly after eating, she had Father take her back home. That was the one and only time Alisa ever met Mother, and the last time I saw her.

Hope Doran

VINNIE

Vinnie was a beautiful soul, masterful at caring for others. I spent our years together being touched by that, wishing Vinnie would be that kind to themselves. They never saw themselves as they presented. I wish they had told all of us sooner. I know there was a period of time where they tried, but I did not see what it was they were saying. Instead, I attributed our conversations to teenage curiosity. I'm grateful that they were finally blunt enough with me so that my thick head got the point. When I finally understood Vinnie had been talking of himself and not just speaking in generic terms, I shifted to accommodate what he was requesting. He became freer with me, more honest with me... more honest with himself after that realization and acceptance on my part. You see he was the son I didn't know I had. I honor him in that and am thankful I got to call him my son, because that is how he had always seen himself.

My beautiful child... It is his death that gave life to this book. That crisp November night when his father called to tell me Vinnie had been in an accident. That was his only detail. Vinnie always lived life on his terms, and those terms were powerful. Vinnie challenged boundaries all the time, so when we asked that he take his ID with him when he went out, Vinnie didn't see the point in that, so he rarely did. It was hours before we knew where he was because he was listed as a Jane Doe.

We hunted for him, driving to the local hospital in hopes of finding him. All the while his dad had been calling local trauma units, finally finding him at a trauma center over an hour's drive away. When we arrived, Vinnie was in surgery. We had no idea what his condition was, but we knew it wasn't good. He had no seatbelt on when the driver, on his cell phone, and driving too fast, lost control of the car, flipping it. Expelled whippets were found in the carnage of the vehicle, but they process through so quickly, it's impossible to test for it in the bodies system. The driver's reckless negligence sent Vinnie flying up the embankment, or at least that's what we were told.

The team of doctors walked like an advancing wall towards us. We held our breath, the three of us, Vinnie's father, Alisa, and myself, all hoping for something that was just not available. Vinnie was broken. They told us they relieved the pressure on his brain but said there was no brain activity. They said that's how Vinnie came to them. They said the possibility was slim for recovery, and there was little hope for him. With that, they retreated like a fog as we took in what was said.

We held each other and cried. We had been forged together over the years. Steeled together by the love we all had for Vinnie. We all wanted what was best for him. Individually we had attempted to swim in the undertow of Vinnie's struggles while navigating his growing into adulthood. We appreciated each other's effort because each had put forth their best. We had become a team in the past years, sharing in the thing called parenting. We had come to do it quite well. In seeking out to do the very best we could by Vinnie, we had bonded together. We were more than just three people; we had grown to be comrades. In that moment we could do nothing but hold each other and wait. We sobbed there, in that space, not caring if anyone saw us. That was our first wave of grief.

The next days were treacherous. The little hope we had vanished, evaporated from the recesses of our "what if" thinking. Vinnie was still there, but in body only. I saw with my own eyes as they checked for life, stopping the assisted breathing to confirm he was not there anymore, only to restart the machines to keep his heart going. You see, in true Vinnie form, always seeking to help better other people's lives he had elected to be an organ donor.

We sat with him for days, keeping watch over him, fighting with nursing staff to stand guard over him so that he was not alone. During those long days, I ushered in friend after friend of his, letting them say goodbye to him, hold his hand one last time, to talk about one silly story or another, regaling me in their adventures as they held Vinnie's hand. Or the more painful visit with the one who came to hold his hand and through a tear-filled face, say they were so, so, so very sorry.

Our friends also came in and Vinnie's company grew as family, friends, both Vinnie's and ours came to be by his side. Our friends sat tirelessly with us in such beautiful, loving support. I was grateful for each and every person that came. Their presence showed their true bonds of family and friendship as the process of life and death was so painful and arduous. We all waited as multiple teams of doctors coordinated to keep Vinnie viable to save lives while finding recipients for his beautiful gift.

The time was so painfully long. The days seeped into each other as we stood watch over him. The doctors did not disclose it would be almost a week before we said our final goodbye to him. It was the worst six days of my life. As things came to a close, I sat with him one last time. I held his hand as tears poured out of my eyes, telling him how very much I loved him. I sat amazed at how little those words actually compare to the vast amount of love that I have for Vinnie, for the beautiful spirit that he possessed. It was so hard to see him, hold his hand, stroke his sweet face, knowing it was the last time. Knowing it was only for me because he was already gone. I held his hand as I kissed his forehead for last time and said goodbye.

The hospital raised a donor flag in Vinnie's honor. The verbal directions to the flagpole were awful, but after some persistence, in the dark morning, we made it. It was a tiny flag that could barely be seen once it was hoisted up under the American Flag. It seemed so trivial watching it floating in the early morning air. It dimmed in comparison to my son's life, and I wept as I watched it retreat down the flagpole and be given to Vinnie's dad.

Hospital staff and the Donor Network team thanked us for seeing that Vinnie's gift of life was honored. The full staff lined the hallway in honor as Vinnie was wheeled out on the bed he had rested on for the past six days. We followed him down to the awaiting ambulance. From there, we stood, among precious family and friends in the crisp, pre-dawn air and watched him go off. In true Vinnie fashion, he was driven away, off to his next adventure, which was to, quite literally, save the lives of others. But not just that, to improve other people's lives, to help advance science, to be the hero he always strived to be. It gives me some small sense of peace knowing his beautiful, courageous heart is beating within a man in Southern California. His liver saved the life of a young woman in her twenties, also in Southern California. I hope to meet them someday. I hope to tell them how truly amazing my son really was.

Hope Doran

MOTHER

This thing called life is delicate, but not as delicate as the relationships within it. I hadn't spoken to Mother in years. It was not for a lack of trying. She was just not available because we had a different set of belief systems. In spite of that, I still always craved that precious relationship with her. Vinnie's death brought to the forefront once again the fact that I had always craved closeness with Mother, forgetting Mother didn't crave that with me.

As I sat, waiting to know Vinnie's status, I was just so desperate to feel a mother's love. I longed to hear comforting words of wisdom that mothers would typically drench their children with during such perilous times. It was in that moment that I thought perhaps; just maybe she would be there for me.

I sat in the cheap vinyl hospital seat as the phone rang in my ear. It was my second call as Father's cell phone went to voicemail. Her voice cut through the phone with a crisp hello. "It's me, mom," I said through sobs. Mother listened, cried, and said she was so sorry. She wept with me as my shaking hand held the phone, telling her what had happened to my youngest child. It was comforting to hear her voice, and in that moment, to feel as if we had found a connection within the tragedy. We hung up with the promise that she would check in with me.

The hospital was a whirlwind as I sought out the friends that I knew were closest to Vinnie. I invited them to come and share one last moment with him. I offered so they could say goodbye. I offered so they could say they were sorry. It was very important to me that Vinnie's friends had that opportunity. I knew Vinnie would have wanted them to have it. I sat with them, consoling friend after friend, wanting to be there for them in their time of need. I didn't think to call Mother because she had said she would call me.

She did call, two days later. She said she had missed a call to the cell phone, and I explained that I had called on the cell number prior to calling on the landline. She was brisker this time, telling me the cell phone did not get good reception, and we moved onto Vinnie's status. I let her know we were in the donation process and told her what we had been told. That was the fact it could take a day or two to align everything up. Everything changed when I told her that she and Father were running out of time to say goodbye.

Mother's cold voice cut through the phone telling me she was too frail to make the trip. I had heard from my brother that she rarely traveled, so I knew that was at least partially true. I had found out that we could have a wheelchair taken out to her so that she could come without having to walk from the parking lot to the ICU room. She tartly said she wouldn't do that.

Then I asked if Father was coming. I was briskly told no. She said she was too dependent on him. She said that the 90-minute trip to Salinas would be too long for her to be without him. I listened to her as the words fell flat in my ears. I knew Father frequently visited my aunt, who lived over two hours away from them. What she was telling me was a lie, and I knew it.

Mother continued on. It seemed as though she was seeking to cut me as deeply as she possibly could. She was passive aggressive as she fired off comments about not having seen Vinnie since she was 10 (not knowing of Vinnie's gender affirmation) and she preferred to remember her that way. Mother said she really didn't know what else to say to me. Apparently, she spoke for Father as well, but I wouldn't know. Even though I called on his line, it had been Mother who responded from those two nights ago. Sometimes I wonder if she even told Father I called.

I asked again for them to come, to be a support, to say goodbye, to have a moment of healing within the family. She again said that would not happen. Mother then said I would have to change too much for that to be a possibility, and I obviously wasn't ready for that conversation. I couldn't believe she was using the fact I was gay as an excuse to not be present; to not be a support to so many that needed them and would have lovingly received them.

I called her out, saying I had been ready for some time… but she cut me off, saying it didn't seem that way by the lack of phone contact. When I started to finish what I wanted to say, she cut me off again, telling me now was not the time for the conversation, and she didn't want one of us to say something we'd regret. She didn't want to hear the truth, her truth, which was that I had reached out on numerous occasions to revive something that was already dead. Interesting that she always did tell me actions speak louder than words. The action of Mother shunning me was obviously something she didn't regret. I wondered if she had even for a moment considered what she had told me with her heartless actions.

I was floored. If I could have reached through the phone and punched her, I would have. Instead, while surrounded by Alisa, Ian, and John, I listened as Mother told me that she and Father wouldn't be coming. Not to say goodbye, not to support her other grandson, not to support her own children. I listened as she told me my lifestyle didn't support her being present in such a dark hour. I sat with tears rolling down my face and told Mother the phone worked both ways before I said goodbye.

They all watched as I sobbed. There was nothing else to do. No words or gestures could fix what happened. We sat for some time, taking in everything that had just transpired, none of us knowing what to say. I now not only grieved the loss of my child, but the loss of my relationship with my parents. It was a blow that was meant solely for me, but it was an action that crushed all of us.

For me, that was my wake-up call. That was when I realized Mother was never going to just be my mom. That is when I realized I had spent over 50 years trying to salvage something that was never there to begin with, never complete, never available, and I'd venture never really desired by her in the first place. I realized I had hidden all these mean, narcissistic events and behaviors in the hopes of having the impossible. That was a real, loving relationship with my mother. I hid all of this at the expense of my own self-worth, my own emotional health, and almost at the cost of my life. I hid my story because up until Vinnie's death, I thought I stood a chance of being worth something to her.

But something changed; I decided I was worth something to myself. I was important enough to tell my story, to set myself free from the dingy silence that had held me hostage all these years. I realized I loved myself enough to be true to who I am. In untangling these few events I have shared from my life; I have found freedom. Hopefully, my story will be a beacon of light to someone else in need of knowing they are not alone. I hope it shows them they are important; they do matter, and they can overcome what they have been born into. Most importantly, I hope they see that they do not have to be a product of their environment, but rather they can create their own canvas in life, and in doing so, cultivate an oasis in the chaos and find healing.

Hope Doran

THOUGHTS

The reality of being a product of a narcissistic parent is that you fit a narrative for them, nothing more. Because of that, you will never be good enough to garner any semblance of real, unconditional love from them. No matter who you are or what you offer. You will never win their love through academic success, having a fantastic, solid career, showering them with love, marrying who they want you to, or even giving them the only grandchildren they will ever have. The narcissist can't have you successful without them because that shifts the narrative from them to you, and they resent that.

Quite simply, you fit a motive for them. When they get what they want, you become a disposable hostage to them so long as you attempt to have a loving relationship with them. They love you for what you provided for them, not for who you are.

I have told my story fully aware it could have been worse. I don't claim to have had the most extravagantly awful story. I only claim to have a damaged childhood, which bled into my adult life for decades. I offer a reason why, and hopefully, an inspiration for others to escape a similar situation. I want people to see that Mother gave me just enough rope to keep me bound to her view of who I was, and how I perceived myself. She hid me from what my real worth was. She led me to believe that if I tried hard enough, I would be whole, and she would love me. That was simply not true, but it did keep me tethered to her.

The truth has been that my life was, and continues to be extraordinary, even with all its imperfections. Even in spite of Mother. My flaws, my successes, they all helped shape me into a person I am proud of. Even the years of blindly voicing my love to Mother ended up helping me gain strength in my own voice. It gave me the tenacity to take that same fierce energy and apply it where I should… in myself.

It is the narcissist who thinks everything around them is dependent upon their approval for survival. I am proof that is not true. I discovered I don't need permission to tell my story, and I hope that others see their path more clearly through our shared experiences.

So, I started with spending my childhood thinking I would be free of Mother when I turned 18. It wasn't until all those years later I discovered I was entangled in the web of pain and lies she weaved throughout the fabric of my life. I survived decades of depression, and lack of self-worth before I was able to set myself free. The fiery trauma of Vinnie's loss was the last piece I needed to obliterate everything Mother had cursed me with believing. That was, if I just tried enough, worked hard enough, sacrificed enough, was godly enough, I would have her love.

Vinnie's last parting gift to me was the sweetness of closure.

www.ingramcontent.com/pod-product-compliance
Lightning Source LLC
Chambersburg PA
CBHW050244010526
44107CB00003B/177